IAN NIALL'S
COUNTRY NOTES

COUNTRY LIFE

IAN NIALL'S

COUNTRY NOTES

OCTOPUS BOOKS

ILLUSTRATIONS BY:

Leonora Box, John Busby, Jeanne Colville, John Francis,
Ros Hewitt, Caroline Holmes Smith, Delyth Jones,
Robert Morton, Barbara Walker

This edition first published in 1987 by
Octopus Books Limited
59 Grosvenor Street, London, England

ISBN 0 7064 3064 6
Printed in Spain by Cayfosa, Barcelona

Contents

Introduction

Long before I was invited to contribute to *Country Life* I was given some advice by J.W. Robertson Scott, master of the art of writing and a great admirer of the famous C.P. Scott of the *Manchester Guardian*. Write as you speak, he said. He was talking about plain English, and I believe he had been told that by C.P. Scott. It made it sound very easy. I remembered what I had been told, and was a little more skilled in the art of writing when I sat down to do my very first set of Notes.

I think the Notes pleased Frank Whittaker, the editor of the magazine. At any rate the only criticism I ever received from him concerned, not my use of words, but a piece I wrote on the adage, be true to an old coat and an old hat, my father's regular excuse for his unsartorial appearance. Readers would be bored to death to hear any more about my old hat and coat. "Get rid of the old hat!" he said, and I did so immediately. After that Whittaker never felt it necessary to guide me. I enjoyed complete freedom to write about anything that came along: the behaviour of birds and animals, my dog, my walks in the hills, fishing, and planting the kitchen garden long used as a henrun.

Successive editors, John Adams and Michael Wright, let me continue in the same way and their encouragement made me feel that I was part of *Country Life*. Week by week, without ever failing to get my material to the editor in all the years I have been writing for this great magazine, I have considered and mulled over my ideas until Sunday morning, when they would come, hot from the oven, in perhaps an hour and a half.

It surprises me to find, after dabbing away at a pocket calculator, that I have written over two million words for this feature alone, and have had almost as many published in book form. The world has been changing all this time and the face of the countryside with it. In my childhood, ploughing and harvesting were long, drawn-out affairs. The tractor-drawn binder was on the field when I was doing my first stint of Notes but it soon gave way to the lumbering combine. Ploughshares multiplied. Fields began to be sprayed. Weedkillers banished the lovely wild flowers of spring and summer from the cornfield and the hedge bank. As I saw change so my outlook changed, too. I had been a keen shooting man. Pangs of conscience made me give up though I could not bring myself to give up my first love, fly-fishing.

I had lived in Wales for something like 40 years when family reasons persuaded us to move south. I shall always miss the mountains. I have a soft spot for Wales. But if it saddens me to think that I no longer hear the raven's early morning call as he flies over the very roof of the cottage I lived in, I can listen to the muntjac barking, and see that bigger, better-nourished fox of the shires who would hardly know his paler Welsh relative. There is a bonus here, too. I feed a score of pheasants who come to the airing green for breakfast every morning, knowing that they will be better fed here than in the keeper's wood. The real blessing of anyone's life is to have done what he loved doing and been paid for doing it. Not everyone is quite so fortunate.

DENIZENS
OF THE
COUNTRYSIDE

Like the word conservation, habitat has a somewhat ominous ring to it for the man who believes that he has the right to do what he likes on his own land. Far-sighted people hold that if present trends continue we will not just be talking of the long-gone day of the bustard on Salisbury Plain and the corncrakes in the meadow; we will find that we have squandered the inheritance that should have gone to our grandchildren.

I often think about the things that have happened in my own time. The red kites I first saw in Wales are certainly not spreading through the principality. In my time the peregrine has declined. We poisoned it, and we polluted the water the otter swam in. In the south, pastureland once beyond the pale has been covered by concrete. The fox might be urbanized, but old Brock could not live in the world of urban man.

Suitable habitat is vital to all creatures. Alas, we rarely concern ourselves with the fact that our own habitat may be threatened by our short-sightedness. Awareness that this is so has made me more and more interested in the natural world around me – the world of which I am a part along with other animals, birds and plants.

November 1971

MY friend who keeps a badger as a pet, was telling me how the creature had come to expect to be admitted to the living room where he fraternised with the family cats, and did his best to establish a friendly relationship with the dog. Dogs are nervous of badgers, I think, because the badger is quite fearless. My friend said that he could scold his pet, whom he calls Humbug, and the badger would stop knocking ornaments off a shelf or poking his nose into some article of furniture he hadn't examined before; but if the reprimand took the form of a slap on the nose, Humbug counter-attacked immediately. The relationship had been briefly interrupted when Humbug had left home and couldn't be found for a couple of days. This desertion may have had something to do with a temporary shortage of baby food, upon which, at this time, Humbug had been accustomed to being fed.

By a strange chance Humbug was located when a telephone call summoned my friend to the home of the local district nurse. Humbug had been scratching at her door. It seemed that he had scented his staple food, which the district nurse kept in bulk in a store cupboard.

While a badger makes a fascinating pet, it has a bearlike blundering way that can hardly be curbed. At tea time, my friend says, Humbug will arrive at the table, rear up and put his strong black forefeet on the edge of the table and expect to be fed. Once he is part of the family the rule is that everyone has equal rights and must share and share alike. How can such a pet be returned to the wild and successfully rehabilitated? The responsibility of taking him into the family is a heavy one, for it is doubtful that his own kind will accept him if he is cast out.

DENIZENS OF THE COUNTRYSIDE

THE leaves haven't gone from our walnut trees, but the nuts have. In other years we always had walnuts, but this year a grey squirrel came down and explored the outermost branches of each tree, taking the nuts one by one. He carried them off to bury them, when he didn't mismanage the thing and let them fall into the long grass. Occasionally he would pose on the asbestos ridge of the garage and gnaw at a walnut, trimming the green ball as he expertly turned it in his paws until it was all eaten, or reduced to fine chips. The whole crop went in about three or four days. I could have discouraged the squirrel with a gun, but he was so impudent that I couldn't bring myself to harm him. Between whiles he went down to the duck's run and helped himself to bread fragments which I had scattered among the barley in the feeding dish. The duck, I could see, was apprehensive of this bold, rat-like visitor. It looked at him, stretching its neck about half an inch from the ground, and never taking its eyes from him. The squirrel ignored the poor duck. When he had had his fill, he would scamper off up the path, returning about the same time next day, taking bread after eating the green walnuts. On the final day two squirrels were there. They haven't shown up since. They must know that the harvest is over. There isn't a nut left on any of the three trees.

HUMBUG, the badger I mentioned not long ago, was given his freedom and released in a wood some miles away from the household in which he had received his infant nurture. For days, although the friend who released him visited the wood and called his pet's name, Humbug buried himself in the depth of the larches and didn't show face. As badgers are nocturnal animals this wasn't really surprising. If he had excavated a hole for himself he was probably lying below ground, snug in bracken or hay which he could have gathered on the adjoining rough ground. Once Humbug had gone walk-about and trundled round the village for a while, but now he would revert to the wild, distracted from his daily routine by the intrusion of humans rather than attracted by them, as he was when living in their midst. The other day the first report of Humbug's homing was received. He had been heard scratching at the door of a house at the other end of the straggling village. He had been seen in the half-light. Soon, my friend fears, he will be knocking at the door. To bring about a speedy reunion my friend would go about calling his pet's name by night, but he is just a little self-conscious about the whole thing. What would a stranger think, coming upon a man in the dark, who continually called Humbug?

DENIZENS OF THE COUNTRYSIDE

MY friend who kept a tame badger and released it into the woods, trusting that it would rehabilitate itself, but found that it "homed" with great determination, is now almost resigned to having it as a member of his household. I saw the badger yesterday. Humbug had only his nose showing from the inside of an old, oval Royal Navy cask. It was the middle of the afternoon, and when I spoke to him, he gave me an unfriendly reception and tucked his nose in. A badger is not to be discouraged once it has joined the family. It belongs even more than the family dog belongs. It will break the door to gain admission. It will not be put out, driven off or punished. I had already come to this conclusion when a letter came from a reader who had some interesting things to say on the subject.

"I am very concerned for poor Humbug", he writes. "Badgers are not suitable creatures for domestication. As cubs grow older, the natural curiosity and tremendous, tireless vigour and power of these animals develops and they become quite impossible in a house. Shut in a room when they want to be outside is simply inviting a hole to be bored through a wooden door in very quick time. Likewise, if a spring squeaks in the seat of an armchair and the badger thinks something should be investigated, the whole seat, springs and all, will be in shreds all over the floor in a couple of minutes – and it is no use smacking him on the nose, as your friend has found out. This kind of experience will soon bring a desire to return him to the wild, which means death, because he will not be able to fend for himself and will be attacked by his kind. Or to contain him in some sort of steel and concrete kennel: the frustration of this will literally drive him mad.

"An acquaintance of mine who has made a great study of badgers and is in frequent demand by television as 'promoter' of live, wild badger shows in wildlife programmes, has the answer to the foregoing problem. Depression of his doormat rings the doorbell and wild badgers have been encouraged to come each evening, ring the bell and receive from him one spoonful only of pretty fruity minced ham. They then go off on their normal wild foraging and are not encouraged to become pets. The journey to and from the door involves passing an artificial and heavily wired badger sett constructed in his garden. In this sett are placed problem children like Humbug – for rehabilitation in safety through the wire, and eventual release to the wild."

Humbug, I am told, is becoming daily more of a handful. A tap on the nose would be repaid with a bite in the early stages of his development. Now such admonition is received with so much ferocity that the person attempting to apply it must run for his life and move as quickly out of the badger's way as he possibly can. Once Humbug lived in the garage in a sort of artificial earth. Now my friend may have to consider moving into the garage and letting Humbug have the house. Rehabilitation has become imperative.

DENIZENS OF THE COUNTRYSIDE

MOST animals, wild or tame, may be seen "playing" at one time or another. Hares will run round and kick their heels for the sheer joy of doing so, even though there isn't another hare in sight, and even the stoat, cold-eyed and vital though it may seem when it is hunting, stops and plays on occasion. I was re-minded of this not long ago when a lady of my acquaintance remarked that she had watched a stoat in her garden. The little hunter had come over a wall and seemed fascinated by a seashell which lay on the side of the path. It took hold of the shell and then dropped it. It picked it up again and began to carry it away. At the wall the effort required to keep a hold on the shell and climb proved too much and the shell had to be relin-quished. After looking back at the lost treasure the stoat returned and attempted to take it through a hole in the wall. It was obviously a much desired plaything. One sees cats doing this kind of thing a lot, and dogs also have their "toys" or playthings.

DENIZENS OF THE COUNTRYSIDE

HAVING a sentimental outlook towards creatures with which one has daily contact produces certain drawbacks and incongruities. For instance, my wife opens the kitchen window and offers shortbread or sweet biscuits to one of the squirrels on its daily begging trip to our door. Squirrels prefer shortbread to ordinary bread, I am told. I offer this information to biologists and zoologists for what it is worth. While they may have guessed that this is so, we have proved it. We have done more. We have educated our squirrels. We have taught them to nibble for a few moments at the slice of ordinary, unbuttered bread we give them and then disdainfully throw down the offering and wait for something better. We might almost call ourselves animal trainers for, believe it or not, while he waits, that begging squirrel puts his right paw on his breast. One might say he supplicates charity with his hand on his heart. This is touching. It is in fact irresistible.

Given the shortbread which I would myself eat with my coffee in the evening, the squirrels go through an almost human display of nibbling. Like zoo apes, they know what they are at. Humans can't resist this imitative behaviour. They are a soft touch, to use the language of the old tramps. With a stick of shortbread half-eaten, the "performer" will scuttle away across the slabs, rush up the limestone wall and pose there on the top of a coping stone. "Any shortbread left?" I ask. There hardly ever is, despite frequent bakings. Shortbread is bad for putting on weight, and squirrels need carbohydrate to see them through the winter, I am informed. All this is very plausible, but I have a feeling that our squirrels aren't being encouraged to put anything away for a rainy day. They know we are always good for a handout. When the time comes and other squirrels are taking a winter nap, even the partial hibernation most self-respecting squirrels go in for, ours will be down, lined up with hands on hearts, going through the ritual. Why shouldn't they, when they know we have endless supplies of shortbread?

The leaves have now fallen, and I can see the ribs of the walnut trees. We have no walnuts at all. Not a single one. The squirrels took them from the trees, not when they were black and hard-shelled, but when they were green and the hulls were succulent. Come to think of it, this probably added a savoury touch to the palate after sweet shortbread, made only with butter. I can't help muttering about this squirrel-feeding, especially when there is a suggestion that we try them with Double Gloucester or Brie. Soon we shall be feeding them pâté and caviare, no less, and then what?

THE grey squirrel never misses a day at the window to beg for food. Her latest delight is in devouring a slab of chocolate cake which is almost a third of her size. She stands holding it between her forepaws and nibbling at it furiously, aware, perhaps, that if she doesn't get it all bolted down, she may be disturbed and have to leave more than half the anticipated feast to be picked up by a thieving gull. What more can a small animal need than this vast quantity of starch, fat and sugar? I am amazed to see that when the enormous lump of cake has been eaten, the squirrel still manages to dash up a tree. Perhaps like many smaller rodents, the squirrel needs a great intake of food to keep it going.

It may be that the steeplejack activity of squirrels burns calories much faster than most animals of like size. On the other hand, to use a Thurber phrase, what we have may be a slothful squirrel, one that lies back content, knowing where the next meal is coming from. Ah well, it serves one purpose. It keeps me from eating chocolate cake until I have taken so many calories that I must lie back and wonder how a squirrel has the energy to climb a tree.

DENIZENS OF THE COUNTRYSIDE

A FIELD MOUSE lives in the henhouse, enjoying the warmth of the deep litter which makes a completely dry and snug cover for his mining activities. Now and again, on damp or wet days, I scatter layer pellets on the litter and the hens have a great time scratching for them. The mouse gets a feed. He isn't at all afraid of the hens, although I am sure the ex-battery birds would make short work of him if he came within pecking distance. He isn't afraid of me, either, because I don't make any effort to pursue him or frighten him away when he trundles along a spar or one of the timbers of the main structure. I could, I suppose, get to know that mouse better, and even make a pet of him. It has been done with house mice and even with field mice, more attractive creatures than the grey house mouse.

I had been thinking about mice and their tameness the other morning on my way down from the henhouse, when the postman came across the court with the morning mail. Among the letters was one from a reader who has adopted a field mouse.

"We have a long-tailed field mouse as a pet – of necessity, for I cannot release her," writes my correspondent. "She was found lying, apparently dead, and no bigger than a bumble bee ... I picked her up, and she immediately came to life ... I carried her indoors, and offered warm, diluted milk in the usual pen filler. The tiny pink hands grabbed this at once. Unfortunately the rubber thing has perished, so I took it off, and tried to regulate the milk with my finger, but made a bosh shot. The little thing got a face full, and wouldn't take milk from that moment. However, she took water, with glucose.

"We didn't expect this extremely groggy little mouse to last the night (I had it in a box by my bed) but without going into the entire history, she is now three months old, small (she must have been the 'runt' and only just emerged from the nest when found) and I am Mum, as she cannot remember her own! She comes into my hand (I hold her tail between a finger and thumb) and sits eating a tiny morsel of cheese (this only offered once a week) or some other food she likes. She's fed on our pheasants' corn, mixed seeds, berries I collect for her, also peas (cooked, and with plenty of sugar!), etc., etc. Little bits of cooked potato, and of course monkey nuts and sunflower seeds. Melon and marrow seeds. If we let her go she would be very soon killed – even by her own kind.

"She lives in an aquarium, a small nest box in one corner, the floor a thick layer of moss peat, some 'tastefully' arranged stones, quite a lot of heather and leaves – and she has made herself a sort of mountain (buries her food) and now, since she seems quite warm when she comes into my hand, and the aquarium has not the least unpleasant smell, I do not clear it and renew it so often as I used to. Her activities are extremely interesting to watch."

January 1975

WHILE I won't say I have a deep insight into the behaviour of animals and the way their minds work, I begin to learn something about the squirrels coming to our kitchen window. For one thing, they impersonate one another at times, while on other occasions they are most careful to establish their identity. The first arrival hops on to the windowsill about half an hour after daylight has come and sits there with hands across her chest, supplicating alms. I go to the biscuit tin. She can hear the rattle of the tin and stands taller, her nose twitching and her eyes as bright as drops of clear water.

The sound of the tin being opened means a sweet biscuit will shortly be tossed on to the garden, which is on the level of the windowsill but separated from the window by a narrow passage. The little beggar always springs from windowsill to garden when the window is about to be opened, quickly picks up the biscuit and runs off with it. I have found that instead of devouring these handouts as she did in summer, perched on the top of the wall, the first-come squirrel now hides the titbit and comes back for more. She will do this three or four times, if I am foolish enough to go on handing them out, but when I stop she goes off and the impersonation begins. Another squirrel arrives and does her best to look as though she has eaten the biscuit I gave out and is still very hungry. I know she isn't the same one. She isn't so fat. I pretend I have been fooled, but soon another one arrives. I know he is not the one I fed before, but he pretends he is.

This morning when the first one came, I found we had no sweet biscuits. I gave out a piece of that cardboard we call crispbread. It fell down into the passageway below. The squirrel dropped down after it and brought it up, but she didn't eat it. Instead, she sniffed at it and put her paws together like an old woman knitting. I began to wonder about the wholesomeness of this stuff. I prowled round the larder and found a tin containing a rich jam sponge (I deny myself such sweet pleasure now that I have got my weight down) and cut the beggar a slice. She couldn't scamper off with it to "hide it in a hedge", but had to eat it there and then. It was too soggy and too crumbly for anything else to be done. The rest of the squirrel tribe came down in due course. I cut them all a piece of sponge. None was able to slip away and hoard the stuff so I suppose I will have a queue tomorrow. They all lurk up there in the trees waiting their turn to come, pleading baksheesh for the love of Allah, or whatever it is they mumble while they sit with paws on chests.

DENIZENS OF THE COUNTRYSIDE

LOITERING comes easily to me. I suppose I was born with a talent for standing at gates, listening to things, staring across fields. Yesterday I was indulging my talent, loitering under a pear tree that grows on the wall while I spied on my bee colonies. When one has bees one can get near to them and guarantee that only the most determined seeker will venture as far. I was not wearing a veil, but I find that bees are singularly unconcerned until they are made aware of the presence of an intruder by some violent action on his part. I was enjoying the drone of the hives and the rustle of the leaves of the pear tree when across my foot passed a shrew, sniffing but not scenting me, and looking as blind as the cartoon character Mr Magoo.

I was fascinated by the pig-like shrew, who was in search of a meal, it seemed. I am not well up on shrews, but I had always fancied they kept under cover in the middle of the day and hunted at dusk or in the dark. They have a short-sightedness that suggests they are not at their best in brilliant sunlight. On the other hand they need a lot of food to keep them going. The shrew came round and inspected or snuffled under a stone close to my foot, and then dived into a thick jungle of grass. I thought that was that, but after a minute or two, when my attention had begun to wander, the shrew came back again and disappeared in the direction from which it had come.

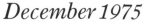

December 1975

MY farmer neighbour has a rather large, doleful, liver-and-white cocker spaniel which tells me when his master is out by barking if anyone passes the farmhouse. Yesterday I met the spaniel on the path beyond the stile. He waited for me and galloped round me, inviting me to accompany him on a walk.

The dog might have been doomed to being a household pet or at best a guard, but he told me quite plainly that he was a hunter and bustled off in front to prove it by putting up three cock pheasants and looking back at me when they rose as though asking what we should have done. He came from the keeper, I recalled, and is of a long line of working gundogs. What is in the blood will out. He hurried on and flushed two more birds, which I was happy to see going safely into a distant wood. We went on up to the limestone escarpment. The dog's doleful look had completely gone.

On the way back we skirted the old lime kiln. He found six more birds in ones and twos. I don't think he had enjoyed himself so much for years. I couldn't help smiling at his delight, but we came at length to the stile. He had accompanied me whatever direction I had taken thus far, but now he stood stock still. The happy look left his face. After a minute he turned and went heavily along the footpath, looking suddenly old again. He would lie by the fire I imagined, twitching occasionally and sighing from the strain of his exertions up on the cliff, and perhaps dreaming of the world he had really been bred for.

DENIZENS OF THE COUNTRYSIDE

SOME interesting comments on the intelligence of animals come to me from a gentleman who lives in Surrey. "I am no expert," he remarks, "but from the two Norfolk terriers we have I have become convinced that their great expertise in always knowing what to do and what is going to happen is because they are very acute observers of the family. First, they seem to possess a very accurate in-built clock (it gets fast at feeding time) and that gets their time table for the day right; second, they watch whoever is around very closely for signs which are familiar to them, getting a windcheater on, picking up the letters on the hall table, laying the dining-room table, etc.; all have a special meaning for them and fit into a known pattern of events. In the same way they watch each other carefully for recognisable signs.

"When they were pups they were seldom more than a few feet apart and seemed to help each other. I remember the first tractor in the field behind: they sat back to back until they had definitely located the noise and then turned to face it and wait till it appeared. This presumably was instinct. Telepathy I used to think had something to do with it, but once when they ran head on into each other round a blind corner I doubted forever after the theory – one was out cold for about ten seconds, the other did a perfect somersault in mid-air and appeared unmoved by the whole accident. There is a healthy competitive spirit between the two – they like to be there first, they must both have a pat and so on – fortunately this very rarely breaks down into bad temper."

THE tangled forelocks of the Old English sheepdog make him a rather endearing sort of fellow, judging by appearances, but the only dog ever to set his teeth in my flesh was an ungroomed, short-sighted animal of this breed. I have never been completely at ease with them since it happened. I was bitten when a boy. Last week I visited the farm where I lived as a child, and there to greet me was the woolly-headed ghost of the dog that bit me. I spotted him out of the corner of my eye just in time to prevent a repetition of the event. The farmer who owned the dog laughed, and said the dog was playful but never bothered anyone. I suppose this was the case. The trouble with me is the Old English sheepdog probably knows I am afraid he will take a lump out of me, and fear is contagious. I am sorry about it, because outside the subconscious, I want to make friends with the shaggy dog. The trouble is that I might end up like some of those people who make well-intentioned attempts to make friends with lions. The shock could be more lethal than the bite.

I don't malign the breed. I just know that I look wrong to short-sighted sheepdogs and it is too late to change that image. I have looked wrong to them for 50 years, although I can't think why. I never saw as much as a hair of the dog that bit me until he had set his teeth in my calf. Perhaps I should have been taken to a psychologist right away? I have thought of putting a note in my diary to the effect that I was nearly bitten by an Old English sheepdog, but if I do there will be a third event.

August 1976

AN early riser I may be, but I draw the line at four o'clock, even if the cock is crowing and the moon still lingering. When something brought me out of my sleep this morning at four I didn't hear the cock and there was no moon. The noise was unusual. I lay a little while trying to think what the whirring sound could mean. The biggest British moth hadn't such a strong wing-beat. It might be a bird, a small bird like a wren? The speculation lasted only as long as it took me to gather my wits and then I knew what the sound was. It was a bat speeding about above the bed and not able to locate the wide-open windows through one of which it had obtained entry. Our bedroom ceiling is unusual. Lying in bed is a little like lying in church, for the plasterwork of the ceiling rises like the nave from the main beams. In this high angle the bat had nowhere to go.

I put on the light but the bat swooped to the bedhead. I knew my sleeping wife wouldn't care to find it doing that so I put the light off again and got out of bed, grabbing my shirt with which I hoped to envelop the frantic creature. People say that a bat locates everything by sending out a high pitched squeak inaudible to the human ear, receiving the echo and reacting accordingly. Well, they may be right, but if they are this particular bat had something wrong with his radar. Twice he collided with the bedroom door and, despite the fact that he made rushes north, south, east and west, he didn't detect the window openings. I think his equipment needed an overhaul. When he had a third collision I dashed in and covered him

with my shirt. He was one of the smallest of bats I have ever handled. Perhaps he was just a beginner. I looked at him in the folds of my shirt and saw that he was none the worse for his head-on collisions with the door. Half asleep, my wife enquired what I was doing and I told her what had happened. She took it all very calmly. Vampires didn't come into her mind. I went to the window, shook out my shirt and the bat was away.

DENIZENS OF THE COUNTRYSIDE

A FRIEND was telling us about the amusing behaviour of her Old English sheepdog, Jolly, when he was little more than a pup. Jolly as a pup was inclined to think that everything was a game. Commands were disregarded. The fun was the thing and his mistress just could not get through to him, however firm she tried to be, until she at last took him and herself off on a course of dog management. Jolly became a most obedient

dog thereafter without being in the least cowed or losing the bright glint of mischief in his eye. On one occasion Jolly's owner was busy washing her kitchen floor using a large plastic bucket and a floorcloth or scrubbing brush. All at once she recalled that it was time for a television programme she watched regularly. She got up from her knees, hurried through the house and settled in front of the television set. After several minutes she was startled to see Jolly coming into the room and steering himself round a large table to present himself at her feet with the large bucket of soapy water firmly held by the handle which straddled his jaws. Was he suggesting she should leave the television and return to her domestic duty, or was he bringing her the soapy water so that she could watch and work in that room?

Some time after this, Jolly began to bring little presents to his mistress. On one occasion Jolly's owner was sitting in a room beyond the kitchen, the door of which opened on to the garden. She heard a great rustling and clatter and after some minutes decided to go through and investigate. Jolly had developed an outsize idea of a present. A large tree had been lopped of its branches, and Jolly had chosen one of these branches as a present. The branch was enormous. It was all the large dog could do to get his mouth round it. The thing filled the doorway completely. It was impossible to bring it into the room, but Jolly was plainly delighted with himself, although he didn't attempt to bring the tree in again when it was removed.

DENIZENS OF THE COUNTRYSIDE

THE plumber has been camping with us for several days, reorganising the radiator layout and fiddling a snake-like device called a sidewinder into the hot-water cistern. Yesterday I noticed him drifting away up the lane. It was really none of my business, but I was curious to know what he was doing. If he had "gone off" us he might leave us in a tangle of pipes and ripped up floor boards. I plucked up my courage and, anxiously studying his face for signs of overstrain, enquired what had lured him up the lane. I need not have worried. The sidewinder had not bitten him. He was not really in a state of nervous tension from not knowing which pipe was which. He had been rehabilitating a hedgehog which he had found in his garden, deciding it might be better off in the undergrowth beside the footpath. His garden was so parched and hard, he had decided the poor hedgehog was starving. He had fed it milk and a special invalid food for several days and felt it might now get by on its own. He is an animal lover. Some weeks ago when he had been working in the attic of a house, he discovered he was due to board in a pair of young feral pigeons. He had rescued the pigeons and brought them home. Hand-feeding both the pigeons and the hedgehog had been quite a task. He still had the birds, but a solution would present itself before long, he hoped.

Returning to the hedgehog, everyone reports a great increase in hedgehog fatalities this summer. Hedgehogs are notoriously ignorant of the highway code. Thousands die on the roads every year, but this summer the drought has hardened up the ground, depriving the hedgehog of worms, beetles and larvae that would normally be found easily. The hedgehog has to forage farther and wider than ever, getting killed in the process.

The rain we occasionally have hardly penetrates the surface of the earth before it evaporates away again, and I am inclined to think the swallows and swifts are going to leave us earlier than usual. They are gathering early. Woodpigeons, short of drinking places and succulent greenery, have returned to my cabbage patch once again, chopping into cabbages and leaving them looking as though they had been munched by a horse. When I took the honey, I found even the bees were waiting for rain, leaving cells uncapped. There are two reasons for combs left unsealed. The honey generally contains too much water and must mature and not ferment. Bees usually seal the comb only when it is ready, but if the nectar supply is short they leave cells open to be filled later. This can be checked by shaking the frame. If honey is scattered from unsealed cells it is not mature. If the honey is not shaken out, the bees are simply waiting to gather more. This has happened this summer much more than it did last year.

DENIZENS OF THE COUNTRYSIDE

NOW that the leaves have fallen from the apple trees in the little orchard, I do not see the squirrels there as often as I used to. For a long time I have blamed the magpie and the jay for the devastation of the sweet apples, and I did so with reason, for when I came up quietly I would often see them gorging on the riper fruit, especially in very dry weather. I was, however, harbouring a viper when I fed the squirrel at the kitchen window. She bred up about three lots each season, and these agile little fellows soon swarmed into the bush apples.

I was lazy this autumn. All kinds of things prevented me from gathering the James Grieve and the Golden Delicious. The squirrels noticed. They found them both quite delicious, and when I went to take my harvest I suddenly saw that there was not one on any of the trees. They, the squirrels, had done my work and I saw them helping the muscovy ducks to dispose of the fruit they felt should not be left on the other trees. They simply knocked the apples off the tree and watched the old ducks rattling down the slope to catch up with them. I am sure the whole relationship was most benign.

The ducks and the old hens love apples, but for some reason the squirrels left one tree entirely alone. It was a Laxton with exceptionally red fruit. The redness may have had something to do with an acute shortage of water. A tree of the same variety did not come through the drought and died in mid-summer.

I have a feeling that grey squirrels are put off by bright red. The apples were as sweet as any others I have tasted this year. One day when I went up I found three young squirrels in the trees at the bottom of the slope. I shouted at them. They all froze on the perch for a moment and then went on with their business. I ran downhill to put them out of that, but all this achieved was the raising of my blood pressure. The small squirrels waited until I was within a couple of yards of the trees they were in and then, dropping to the ground, skipped across to the wych elms, as light on their feet as anything I have ever seen. They certainly have not much weight to carry. The moral of the story is that it is the early squirrel that takes the apple. A man who wants his harvest must make time for it. I cannot shoot all the squirrels I have been largely responsible for by feeding their mother.

March 1977

MOST people who keep animals know they show signs of desolation when they are deprived of company or playmates. What we call mourning seems to take place when, for instance, one of a pair of dogs brought up since puppyhood meets its end. A friend who recently lost one of her Aberdeen terriers, met me in the lane the other day with the surviving dog and said she was pleased to say that the long period of dejection was over. The survivor was no longer mourning. There are, of course, countless examples of dogs apparently mourning the loss of their master. By the nature of things dogs tend to be "fixed" on one person more than another. When that person dies the unfortunate animal is slow in accepting a new idol. My grandfather's dog mourned him pitifully. My father's dog became a runaway and was, I think, disturbed for the 14 years he survived him. Cats, too, apparently mourn.

A reader who had two Siamese cats of very contrasting character writes to tell me a moving story of what happened when one of her pair died. The cats were called Suzu and Sirikit. "They slept on my bed at night," says my correspondent. "Suzu would hunt. Sirikit loved to find playthings and would become anxious if Suzu was absent for more than eight hours. She would sit watching, waiting and worrying. Suzu did most of Sirikit's washing for her. Once when Sirikit had a septic paw and chose the linen cupboard as her sick-room, Suzu, bored but staunch, never left her by night or day, even accompanying her down to the kitchen and garden and attending sessions with the vet. Though Suzu loved Sirikit, she also loved me, whereas Sirikit loved only Suzu.

"During the summer of 1975 Suzu became desperately ill. One day the vet advised ending her suffering. When I came back, Sirikit met me in the hall. I was crying, and Sirikit, sitting in the basket on top of her dead sister, gave me a long look of remarkable sorrow and sympathy. The assembled family were astonished at this look which we have never seen in any animal's eyes before or since.

"Sirikit roamed the house and garden, not searching, but mourning with deep-throated howls. She comforted me, as these cats will when we are in trouble. She even brought a live mouse on to my bed, but to my eternal shame my reception of the kind gift was not what it ought to have been. She never repeated it. When she was alone she wailed. She grew thin, she slept badly, starting and moaning. She sat for long hours under the tall yew trees a few yards from Suzu's grave.

"After three months she rallied, grew more affectionate and settled back into the routine. Later on, hoping to provide company for her, we introduced two sealpoint kittens, but she became miserable and unapproachable and clearly detested them and we had to part with them.

"Sirikit is a beautiful and fit cat again now. She rarely hunts. She never plays. Whatever the weather, she spends all day under the yews."

DENIZENS OF THE COUNTRYSIDE

July 1977

THE shepherd had parked his Land-Rover shortly before I arrived and he was unshipping his dogs to go up the mountain when I drew in. He waited so that he might have company and some conversation on the way up the track, and I remarked that one of his four dogs seemed unwilling to get out of the truck. The reluctant dog was grey-whiskered, a gentle-looking animal well past its prime. The shepherd smiled as he looked at the dog. Too old now, she was. She only came for the ride and she would sleep on the floor of the vehicle after a while, and wait for her master's return. She would not be left at home. It seemed she liked the ride and took a great interest in everything she saw on the way up, whether the livestock happened to be lambs and ewes streaming over the road, or stolid store cattle who simply stood there, too thick-headed or too obstinate to be moved until dogs were unloaded. I found the story quite touching. Even a sheepdog accepts retirement with a certain reluctance, it would seem.

The shepherd was going up to "drive up", which is something hill shepherds do here for days after they have put their flock on the mountain. Until the grazing is good, flocks tend to gravitate to lower boundary walls and gateways leading back to the valley where the feed was good. The hill shepherd diligently drives his flock uphill until they discover the bite. Unless this is done, the grazing close to the boundary and round the gates is over-worked and the grass roots begin to die in a warm spell.

August 1977

REMEMBERING the misfortunes suffered by animals which stray on to the highway, a reader writes to say that she has befriended and made a companion of a weasel. My correspondent tells me that her weasel loves to play, makes "conversation", and enjoys hide-and-seek. He is only seven inches in length, three years old, and very affectionate. When the little creature goes outside he will respond if called. His reactions are very fast and he can throw himself into the air, springing a yard from the ground.

I have known a wild polecat to be semi-domesticated and used like a ferret to catch rats, but it was never in any real sense tamed. Ferrets make even better pets than domestic cats, if one can bear their odour, but the little weasel is a very different handful and I have never before heard of one being tamed. The story is quite fascinating.

December 1977

MY neighbour's dog, a springer spaniel, acts as sentinel whenever his family are away from home. The outbreak of barking tells me that someone is in the farmyard or walking along the footpath behind the farmhouse. The other morning I became aware of barking closer at hand than usual. The farm is getting on for half a mile from us, though the farmhouse itself is somewhat nearer. I thought about it for a while, wondering if someone was trying to break in. It was market day and my neighbour would be off there at the stock sale. His children were at school. I could "see" some housebreaker at work on the back door and made up my mind to go and investigate. I had just got my boots on when it struck me that the bark wasn't the springer's bark but a much deeper one. Nevertheless, I told myself, you must go up the footpath and over the stile and make sure, so off I went.

When I reached the stile I could just make out the head of a very large labrador poking up from the other side of the stone wall. He was very distressed. When I mounted the stone slabs that serve as steps he yelped and wagged his tail frantically. My imagination got to work once again. He was the faithful companion of some old person who had gone for a walk along the footpath and tumbled into what we call the clay hole, which is really a hole from which limestone was excavated to be burned in a kiln on the side of this minor quarry. The dog galloped in front of me as we went to the rescue, but no one had fallen into the clay hole. I began to understand what it all meant at last.

The labrador was adolescent and not very bright. He had somehow got over the stile in the beginning and now couldn't work out how to get back again and return home, so I got him over with a few heaves and shoves. He was much too heavy to be lifted six feet. Once back on the right side the foolish animal dashed about like a mad thing. I told him to go home and he bustled off, swinging from side to side as he went, and very pleased with himself. Things like this underline my conviction that animals vary in their mental ability as much as human beings. Before listening to what a dog seems to be saying one should take a good look at him and make sure he really has all his wits about him. Some are just not as bright as others.

DENIZENS OF THE COUNTRYSIDE

January 1978

A FEW months back I wrote about the old sheepdog's journey to the moorland pasture. A reader writes to give a similar account and it seems that old sheepdogs, like old soldiers, never die but simply fade away.

"Your remarks brought vividly to my memory an old sheepdog whom I knew as a small child," my correspondent remarks. "When Old Gem could no longer streak over the fells she was retired. She had been a wonderful dog, working hard for her masters as had her ancestors before her and as do her descendants today; and she loved her work. Now, small, neat and grey-muzzled, she watched the work of the farm and lay in the sun. Sometimes she disappeared. We all knew where she went, but no one commented. She went to a flat pasture top, below the fell wall and above the cliff that over-hangs the farm, where a few sheep were grazed, and where she could not be seen from the farm. There she worked with the sheep, dividing them, penning them, extracting one from the bunch. Concentratedly, slowly and accurately she would perform her manoeuvres, all alone. One day she brought them all down the beck to the farm gate and left them there. Not having seen her do this, and startled at seeing sheep where no sheep should be, I told the shepherd. He looked, smiled, and turned away. 'Yon's t'Old Gem's', he said. She put them back next day."

March 1978

A LADY writes to tell me how her highly intelligent cat would spring up and claw the sash to bring down the window and gain entry to the room beyond, providing the catch had been left off for him to manage this feat. Cats do seem to have a kind of mechanical knowledge for I have seen one jump up and operate a lever door handle. Friends who have Siamese testify to this peculiar intelligence in the breed. Dogs occasionally manage something of the sort, but they are generally trained to do the "trick" where a cat seems to work it out for itself.

Learning from experience is natural in all animals. A pig learns to open a gate by rooting under it with its snout, and I have known horses to lift a wire or a chain. Susy, our Cairn terrier, clawed the door to have it opened for her. When it was off the catch she would force it back with a great thud against the wall, but alas, although I tried very hard, I could never train her to turn around and close it after her. There was no incentive for her to learn the trick, I suppose.

Long ago when my grandfather would come home from the town a little the worse for wear, his pony would open gates and bring the gig through, but the family were always dismayed when he did, for almost invariably a lot of stock trotted off through the unclosed gate and had to be gathered up the following morning. Both the old man and his "clever" pony were always highly unpopular for a day or two.

DENIZENS OF THE COUNTRYSIDE

YESTERDAY was not the sort of day I would care to experience very often in the future, for I drove 300 miles in order to face the television camera for roughly two minutes' filming on a farm at the far end of Wales. Nine hours of driving is more than is recommended at a stretch but there was, of course, a break in the middle while I spoke my two-minute piece necessary, the producer told me, to establish my identity as the commentator on a film about the old ways of cultivating land. Television producers are fussy about background. Cameramen are too.

It was decided that I should say my short piece in a field where there were about 12 Shire horses, for I was going to talk largely about the horse. Alas, the fine Shires would not come to the camera and after they had ignored the encouraging noises the crew made for them someone went off and got a bucket of oats. We were surrounded by horses in no time. The drawback was that they wouldn't stand still. My "take one", would have been perfect but for the fact that one of the horses nudged me in the back. On "take two" the sound man said the small radio microphone I was wearing was picking up some intestinal rumblings emanating, I assured him, from the horse that was looking over my shoulder. At "take three" the cameraman himself shouted "Cut!" because one of the horses decided that its best side was its hind-quarters. It displayed its "best side" at my elbow. "Take five" was marred by the drone of an aeroplane. By the time we got to "take six" the wind was blowing into my jacket. The sound man insisted we moved from the open part of the field to the shelter of the wall along the lane. "Take seven" failed because the Shires, who had moved with us to the hedge, decided to go back down the field. The bucket of oats brought them back. At "take eight" I think it was the snapping sound of the clapper board that caused a minor stampede. The young man putting in the board was finding it rather trying. I think he was afraid that one of the Shires would set its teeth in his rear end as he hurried to get "out of shot". I wasn't exactly at my best at "take nine" and fluffed my two or three sentences, but "take ten" was marked for printing and "take eleven" was marked too, just in case "take ten" was somehow not technically right. We broke for lunch at this point. I waded out of the mud leaving the Shires with their heads turned, watching me go and wondering perhaps, what that had all been about. I used to think that it was his sour nature that made W.C. Fields say he would never appear with children or animals. Both are unpredictable of course. I felt that what should have been happening was a film of the whole thing by a second camera, from start to finish. It would have been hilarious, even without a series of retakes of the retakes.

DENIZENS OF THE COUNTRYSIDE

A LADY who lives in California and rather belatedly came upon my remarks about animals closing doors after them writes: "Our unusually intelligent golden retriever, Saxon, closed the door behind him after I complained to my husband. 'It's all very well for your dog to open the door and come in, but I wish he would close the door behind him.' My husband said, 'I'll tell him about it.' About 15 minutes later my husband said, 'Alright, he'll do it after this.' Outside, Saxon nudged the door open as he had done many times, and came in. The door swung back against the wall; Saxon nosed the door about half-way shut, then put up his right paw and with a gentle but firm push closed the door. From then on he almost always closed the door behind him without being told; if he neglected doing it in his eagerness to get in I would call to him, 'Saxon, you've forgotten something' and he would immediately come back and close the door. His sister Susy watched her brilliant brother with admiration but never tried to imitate him. Some years later, after the death of my husband, I settled in Carmel. A few days after moving into the house, I looked out of the window and saw Saxon take the iron ring of the gate cord in his mouth, stretch back with it and open the gate and go out. More extraordinary things could be told about Saxon. He conversed at some length, his voice rising and falling and his eyes fixed directly and intently on the person he was 'talking' to. At intervals he paused, and one had to reply in order to keep him talking. I always felt that I knew what he was saying."

YESTERDAY I was walking in town when an elderly gentleman came rushing up to me to ask if I had seen a dog with a joint of meat between his jaws. It seemed the dog had taken a fancy to a lump of beef in a carrier bag put on the ground while the gentleman made some adjustment to his hat. The unfortunate victim confessed that both the meat and the dog were his. He stood looking up the empty street. "Of course it's more than he will be able to manage, fool that he is!" he said, "and more than I can afford – £4.50 worth of beef! You would think he would have more sense!"

Sorry though I was for the man, I could hardly conceal a smile. I remembered something similar happening long ago when a family dog, notorious for his waywardness, suddenly sprang from the floor on to the dining table and made off with a hot, newly-roasted turkey. What a hue and cry there was, but Tweed must have had his line of escape well planned, for he got clean away with his prize. The family had stuffing, potatoes and some green vegetables for dinner. Tweed stayed away for two days and when he returned he slunk in under the kitchen table to hide between the legs of the ploughman and the stockman.

"I'll thump him," the old gentleman promised, as he set off back the way he had come, his carrier bag, with nothing in it, flapping against his leg. "I'll knock seven kinds of dirt out of him!" But I could tell from the way he said it that the dog's punishment would be nothing so drastic.

DENIZENS OF THE COUNTRYSIDE

WHEN I see a horse alone in a field I am always tempted to call to it or go over and see the animal, a temptation I resist, knowing that owners of horses don't always welcome their being visited or made up to. The other day I was standing at a field gate when a rather elderly nag came ambling up to greet me. I was about to put my hand out and pat his shaggy old head when his owner drifted into the gateway on a bicycle and gave me a timely word of warning. It seemed the apparently friendly old horse had a quirk of character. He was inclined to bite the hand that fed or patted him. His long, yellow teeth would clash together like a bear trap. His owner said he was getting worse in his old age. All the world was queer, he said, save me and thee.

Some of us are well aware that dogs and horses have distinct personalities; it would also seem that they have a sense of humour. You will not believe this, of course, unless you know and love dogs and horses. I have known my share of both and I was grateful for the warning from the owner of the old horse. I once knew an old horse that just couldn't resist tipping a man's hat over his eyes, and another that took the buttons off overcoats. A dog we had loved used to bait a Galloway bull who was, in the ordinary way, a most docile beast but in five or ten minutes would be lumbering about, pawing the ground, swinging his tail and bellowing in rage.

I am not sure that cats have a sense of humour but our cat Topsy knows how to get me going by slipping into my office and knocking my fly-tying stuff about if I happen to have left a cock cape or a peacock's feather lying around. As soon as I come to investigate she makes a four-footed set, switches her tail like the old Galloway bull, and rushes downstairs. I am invited to chase after her, but she never smiles. Hers is a kind of black humour.

Susy, our Cairn, always had a distinct way of letting me know I was being dull. She would bounce and bark at me until I came to play and would then exhaust herself and me before she retired from the scene. Horses, too, sometimes invite one to join in the fun but they are choosy about their friends. The old horse that came to the gate was in his crabbed old age. Perhaps it had dawned on him that he had been exploited all his life and he was trying to get his own back.

June 1981

WHEN we go away for the day we have to make provision for feeding and locking up hens, and a neighbour generally obliges us by doing these chores.

At the weekend when I called on my neighbour his face lit up. Could I perhaps do something for him? Like tethering out his goat and shutting it in his shed at the end of its stint of lawn-mowing? I am not a goat person, as they say, not because I don't like goats. They just haven't come my way very often. I had only to lead my neighbour's goat out to grass where he would be secure at the end of his tether. I was up bright and early the following morning and hurried along to meet the goat. He bleated when he saw me through the shed gate. I apologised for being too early or too late. He danced on his back legs and tried to butt me with a sideways jerk of his head. He didn't smile but looked as grim as an ayatollah. I got hold of the rope and sidled past him and he went out through the gate as though released from a stockade.

I floundered behind him, feeling I should have had a stetson hat in one hand so that I could play the part properly. Billy stopped playing up and I fixed the clip in the tethering loop. He watched me go, chewing on a twig that made me think of a white-bearded Kentucky gambler smoking a cheroot. At night he went into the shed quietly and bleated at me as I departed. This morning he had decided I would do. I found myself scratching his head and wondering if I should have spent all that money on a new grass-cutter (it cost eight goats).

DENIZENS OF THE COUNTRYSIDE

MY good intentions, when I think about them, make me ashamed at my lack of perseverance. For years I have intended to keep a record of the birds and mammals I encounter on this patch of ground. Periodically I list them from memory, but that isn't the same as setting down something as and when it happens.

This thought came to me again during the week, when a stoat came lightly up the grass slope and snaked his way into the undergrowth at the top. He wasn't hunting, it seemed to me, but passing through. He hadn't time to wait and catch one of our commonest residents, the field mouse. If I listed the mammals according to their population, then the field mouse would certainly top the list and shrews might come before voles.

Moles would be well down the scale. They make a lot of mounds, but two or three moles are all that are needed to do this. The grey squirrel, like the stoat, passes to and fro. There are a number of old dreys in the pines, the biggest of these being right above the potting-shed gable.

Weasels sometimes scuttle across the lane. They always seem to move at top speed across open ground and hunt in the hedge bottom. I have seen only one hedgehog here and he seemed bewildered and out of his element in a conifer wood.

Rats, like the squirrels and stoats, are visitors. I think they come by when the farmer lower down clears up his barn after all the barley has been milled to feed his cattle. Rabbits show up from year to year. They aren't really residents, and, of course, the hare picks his way across the cliff from one little patch of fine grass to the next, and I think the fox may lie up there in the gorse at times. He "leaves his card" anyway, and when the snow was here he also left his tracks when he sniffed round the locked henhouse.

A badger comes for a while, having a secret gateway somewhere along the top wall in the shelter of a briar tangle. His route appears to be a kind of bypass used for a month or two, perhaps because he finds something to root for in the jungle. He leaves a soiling scrape, and it might be possible, by studying this, to tell just how many nights in succession he comes our way.

There isn't any bigger animal to come. I can't really include sheep or ponies. We did have a couple of ponies here for a short time. They came over the back wall. Their owner arrived and asked permission to search the thicket for them. I went with him and "walked" one of the ponies right down the cliff face by its forelock. I was rather pleased with myself at doing that.

DENIZENS OF THE COUNTRYSIDE

IWAS down in Buckinghamshire recently, looking at my late father-in-law's house, when I found myself summoned from the attic where I had been inspecting the plumbing, because we had a caller. Cob-webbed and in need of a bath, I apologised for my appearance and explained where I had been. Our caller smiled and enquired if I had glisglis. Now there was a thing! For the life of me I couldn't think what a glisglis was. It sounded like some kind of mental trouble that makes a man hide himself in the far corner of attics. My puzzlement showed and I was told a glisglis is a fat-tailed dormouse.

Well, no one can be expected to know everything and up here in North Wales any kind of dormouse is comparatively rare. The fat-tailed dormouse was, I believe, introduced to Britain by the Rothschild family and quickly established residence in properties in the locality in which it won its freedom. It is a creature that likes fruit. Apples stored in a loft are irresistible. It is as hard to keep out as a bat or a grey squirrel when it finds a hole big enough to squeeze through. I went back up to the attic and took a good look round but there wasn't a sign of glisglis. Our caller had also mentioned another "pest", the little Chinese deer muntjac which my wife had earlier seen on the lawn. This miniature deer has begun to spread north, although it hasn't as yet come to Wales.

DENIZENS OF THE COUNTRYSIDE

IN addition to my own chores this morning I performed a couple for my neighbour who is away on holiday. I went to peg out his goat and feed his rabbit. The goat stood on her back legs and did a kind of dance for me, nodding in my direction and showing me the tips of her horns without seriously attempting to butt me. I apologised for the hassle we had had last night, when I was forced to pull her up to a bush round which she had twisted her tethering rope, and presented her with a large Scotch thistle which I had cut on my way along. She set about eating the thistle without delay.

The rabbit didn't wait for the large bunch of clover and damp grass I pulled for him, but thumped the bottom of his cage and dived into his private quarters where he stayed until I was out of range. The goat bleated and acknowledged me as I withdrew. I was almost back at the cottage before I was quite myself again, for if someone had come along in the meantime and offered to sell me a white goat I would have had one. A man must recognise his weakness if he can. For 20 years I have been thinking of having a goat. Perhaps there is an organisation that caters for people with my problem, an official I can ring, even in the middle of the night, and talk it all out? I really must not have a goat for I have a secret horror of walking off in a dream accompanied by a whole herd of them.

AN old great-uncle who used to get bran from the distillery as a supplementary feed for his pigs often used to say that if he fed the bran to his sows too soon after he bought it, the poor creatures got the worse for wear and fell into a drunken stupor. My great-uncle's concern for his pigs used to make a great-aunt look heavenwards and shrug her shoulders at a kind of pot-calling-kettle-black thing, but I did once see the sows inebriated and they were certainly a funny sight. Inebriation is almost always a source of amusement to those who stand soberly watching its effects. In the case of animals it is certainly anthropomorphism that promotes our amusement. We see the animal as human when it staggers, lies down, dazed and not sure where it is. My great-uncle's pigs were not the only ones to become legless, for his old horse also had a liking for bran with a residue of foreshot in it, and it sometimes had great difficulty staying upright and pulling the cart the last few hundred yards into the steading.

This comes to mind after reading about currawongs (Australian birds similar to our magpie) that got drunk on naturally fermented hawthorn berries. According to a report in a Melbourne paper, a passer-by saw currawongs tumbling out of the treetop. Because it was thought the birds were dying, a wildlife officer was summoned, and he, after a brief examination of the paralysed birds, pronounced them drunk. Eventually, the currawongs came to, recovered their balance, and by evening were back in the tree for another session.

July 1983

MY labour clearing undergrowth has uncovered beds of lying-up places used by muntjac during the day. Our small deer are here all the time, but in such cover that they have ample time to move without being seen. Now a good part of the sheltering weeds and tall grass has been destroyed, not only by my labour in the wilderness, but by the tractor-mower in the paddock area. The deer have only close-growing shrubbery and cherry saplings in which to secrete themselves. That they remain means such cover is more to their liking than the woodland adjoining our ground, and is certainly more secluded than pastures in the immediate vicinity.

In the beginning the appearance of deer on the lawn was more frequent than it is now. The muntjac had been accustomed to having the place to themselves. My activity of cutting back and extracting dead trees may have forced them into the more dense undergrowth. Now we see them only at intervals and speculate, between times, on whether they have deserted us.

Last evening we had a rare treat. First a young deer came across the lawn and began browsing on the leaves of cut-back rose trees and was followed by both parents, the horned male bringing up the rear and moving the youngster on with a gentle nudge when it dallied by the fence. The female then took herself and her offspring down the drive and round the clump of spruce trees. The male, after he had gone out into the paddock to feed on a briar rose, plodded on behind them, and all three

were finally lost to sight. I know little about deer of any kind. As a small boy I generally saw them at a distance. Red deer came down on to the farm in late autumn and fed on swedes and took mouthfuls of hay from ricks, but they never stayed long enough for me to get close to them. When disturbed they virtually sailed over hawthorn hedges and drystone walls, covering hundreds of yards in a minute or two. In Wales, when the odd stag escaped from private parkland and got a mention in the local newspapers from time to time, it was heard of no more because some trigger-happy lunatic would lie up for it in scrub and blast it with a shotgun. In this part of the world there are trigger-happy people too. The muntjac is shot.

Fallow deer, advertised by road signs where the road crosses a local common, may be in equal danger, but one hopes not. The other morning, setting off on a fishing trip at daybreak, I was delighted to have to "beware of deer" when two beautiful dappled fallow deer fawns stood on the road watching my approach. At the last minute they swung round and tripped across the verge into mist-hung trees.

It seemed to me a good thing that the average man stays in bed in the morning at least until six, for the world is all the more enchanting at this time of day for his doing so.

September 1983

PERHAPS it was inevitable that once we had the paddock fence down the side of the lawn, we would follow the local trend and have yet another division, a second fence and then a third, two paddocks and finally, three.

The flail was brought in because willow herb was about to seed. Brambles flailed last year seemed to have taken a new lease of life after being pruned. Worse than this, my neighbour's ponies would have waded in a shoulder-high growth without getting at the grass buried by the trampled willow herb. So now we have three paddocks all looking a little the worse for wear. The one near the house has been cropped bare and scorched by the sun. Just in time to prevent the ponies tearing out the shrubbery beyond the wire, we had them moved into the flailed area to munch on a succulent growth of dwarf convolvulus, which they love.

I seem to learn more about ponies every day. They can be most wayward animals. The smallest of the two bays is quite a character. He must have had some circus training, for the other day he trotted out of the spruce thicket to me and raised a hoof like a dog offering a paw. He wanted an apple or a carrot, it seemed. Always a sucker for this kind of thing, I hurried indoors and got a couple of carrots. The small bay, whose name is Rupert, offered a hoof for each carrot. He certainly has me weighed up, for now he lifts a foreleg whenever he sees me and gets his reward, but I feed him furtively, not wanting to be caught depleting the fruit bowl or the vegetable rack.

Another thing I discover is that light-coloured ponies seem more prone to skin troubles than dark ones. Raz, who is a very pale Palomino if not a creamy horse, has had a swollen leg, and the vet had to come to administer injections and apply ointment. Could this be "mud fever"? I was consulted because I might have come across it long ago. The vet himself doesn't need my not very reliable recollections of what happened with work horses half a century ago. The Clydesdales were groomed night and morning and never left to stand out on muddy ground or among uncut, wet grass.

Pony people love their animals and lavish great care upon them, but the old-time horseman looked after his charges with much more vested interest. They were his livelihood. He watered, fed and groomed them and lived with them if he found them ailing. It wasn't his hobby.

DENIZENS OF THE COUNTRYSIDE

IT should have been obvious that the ponies were stripping more and more bark off trees because they were finding less and less to graze on the dry and sun-burnt paddock, but I blamed the bays. They, I thought, hadn't been exercised enough, and they were morbid. Morbid dogs gnaw wood. Morbid pheasants become feather-pickers and, when they draw blood, inflict serious injuries on one another. I thought no more about it, however. The barking of a minor copse of cherry saplings didn't really trouble me.

I might have gone on thinking that what was happening was due to the morbidity of the bays until one morning when I looked out at the lawn I saw Pickles, a small brown pony, trotting across it. How had he managed to get out of the paddock, and what was he doing on the lawn? He was looking for greener pastures. I hurried out in my dressing gown and slippers and plodded after him. The dew drenched my feet before I came up with him. He stopped and allowed me to take his halter, but would he move?

Nothing I could do would persuade him to take a step forward or to be backed. Checkmate, he seemed to be saying, let go of my halter. I had to let go and went back to the dining room for a couple of Golden Delicious. Pickles can't resist dessert apples. He knows the difference between an eating apple and a windfall cooker, which probably has a sour scent for he won't even take one from my palm. But he took the dessert apple, although he stood like an obstinate donkey until I held the second apple in front of him and retreated.

We crossed the lawn in this fashion, and I finally got him through the little gate and into the field. I closed the gate as he trotted away to the far side. Five minutes later he was back on the lawn and this time he came to me for an apple. I put him into the field and hurried to his escape point before he got there, just managing to close the gap in time. The sun was coming up and, I told myself, God was in his heaven, but I was only half dressed when Pickles appeared for the third time. He had sprung the staple from the fence post and got under the wire.

The other ponies are too tall to manage things like this. The message is plain. The second paddock has to be completed and all four animals put where there is more for them to eat. In the meantime they are being given hay and a can of oats to stay their hunger. They have such healthy appetites that every one of them may break out if they don't get their bellies filled.

September 1983

WHEN ten years ago, our much loved Cairn terrier was mercifully put down in her sixteenth year, she was buried that evening by torchlight on the slope above the courtyard of the cottage in which we lived. A month or two afterwards I got a thick block of slate and painstakingly recorded on it the date of the interment and her name. She wasn't buried in a casket or coffin, but in the knitted blanket she loved to have in her bed.

I remember even now the anguish we both underwent. For at least a year afterwards, whenever I got up in the night, I found myself stepping over a little dog who wasn't there. She loved to sleep on the carpet in our bedroom directly over a pipe that took hot water to a radiator. She sleeps on, for the long sleep is not exclusively for mankind, and after ten years we moved. I recall taking a last look at the small slate headstone at the foot of the pine tree on the slope above the court. Susy's bones rest there, but her name and the date will mean nothing at all to the people who bought the cottage. How are they to know that she was the dog of our life, and so much loved that we swore never to have another.

We could never go through that kind of trauma again. Bones are only bones. Ashes to ashes and dust to dust, the ritual insists, and it wouldn't have entered my head to have had poor Susy's remains disinterred, however decently, and removed to Buckinghamshire where we now live. It would have been a morbid exercise. I laugh at myself all the time, but this would have made everyone laugh at me, and my self-respect would have crumbled.

It seems that I may be out of touch, ignorant of the mores of my own or the younger generation, for in some parts of the world they wouldn't have laughed, but looked askance at me for not having my dog dug up and re-buried in Buckinghamshire. In America, where trends are set, a woman who lost her dearly loved cat insisted upon its being buried in a casket at a cost close to £2,000 (my authority, the *Los Angeles Times*) and then, when her husband found a new post in Massachusetts, had the casket dug up and moved east at a cost of about £1,000. Finally the husband was lured back to California. Faced with a similar bill for the disinterment of the cat, he wrote to the *Los Angeles Times* to explain his dilemma. He protested at having to spend so much of his hard-earned salary on digging up the cat and having it moved wherever he went.

Well might he protest, but I see the light myself this time. What if this became a general rule and people felt it necessary to have deceased husbands (or wives) dug up and moved to their new place of residence? Here the Home Office would have something to say about it, but how the undertakers would rub their hands and how busy the clergy would become, and wouldn't local authorities have to think again before making gravediggers redundant.

DENIZENS OF THE COUNTRYSIDE

WE have several nocturnal visitors apart from the bats that haunt the house, one going into a mousehole where the "ceiling" of the porch adjoins the brickwork of the wall. We have an occasional visit from a badger. The fox has his own paths across the lawn, and I detect his entry place in the hedge on one side and his exit in the brushwood on the other. Owls advertise their presence on damp nights, and we enjoy listening to their call echoed from high beech trees on the far side of the lane.

One nocturnal creature I have seen no sign of as yet is the hedgehog. Hedgehogs are almost certainly the commonest casualty on the roads at night until they take themselves into warm holes and leafy nests, living most of the time on their fat. We don't seem to have them here and didn't have them in North Wales, probably because they prefer deciduous woods rather than pines. I was talking about hedgehogs to a visitor the other day, and he had an amusing story to tell about a hedgehog at his door.

The family had been intrigued to find milk bottles rolled away time after time, and had occasionally heard the sound of a bottle rattling, but hadn't been able to solve the mystery until, one night, hearing bottles being knocked over, my visitor had rallied his family. The door was quietly opened. Someone stood by the porch light ready to switch it on, and the head of family, having armed himself with a powerful torch, rushed out to investigate. On the word of command there was

light. The beam of the torch spotlighted a hedgehog, and every one watched, fascinated, as the performance went on. The hedge pig was rolling milk bottles with his snout, apparently for amusement. They were perfectly clean milk bottles, newly scaled with hot water, and the only explanation for the hedgehog's odd behaviour was that it was playing.

All animals play, whether they are domestic or not. A keeper I know once watched a lamb playing with a fox, and it seems that a hedgehog, too, must have its fun.

DENIZENS OF THE COUNTRYSIDE

WHAT is in the mind of a fox that starts to cross the paddock and stops in mid-stride with a forefoot raised, as one did this morning, staring into the sun? After half a minute the fox turned about and unhurriedly took himself back in the direction from which he had come. It wasn't that he had forgotten something, or even, I think, that he had scented danger. He had heard something that quite positively suggested he would be safer heading back, for the fox has a better hearing than most quadrupeds, even if he always takes care to travel upwind so that he can test the scents that come to him.

The fox coming into the paddock had stopped to listen. I could see the fringe of hair that formed a halo round each ear and the set of those ears gathering small sounds which his brain sorted before he made up his mind to go back. Would it not be wonderful to have such senses, to be able to hear such small sounds and differentiate between one sound and another? It might, of course, be painful at times, and quite unnerving, and this may be why a fox turns back into the more remote countryside in which disturbances are few and far between.

Framed in the gap between one of our paddocks and the next, the fox was a picture that remained in my mind after he had disappeared. He turned back, and I could only imagine how he retraced his steps along what was, no doubt, his own familiar trail, something a practised eye could follow but a casual observer would fail to detect.

A RIME of frost covered the barbed wire and the trees on the far side of the first paddock yesterday morning. It was the coldest morning we have had here yet. The horse's water trough was frozen and when I broke the ice it immediately froze again. I couldn't break the ice on the birdbath because it was solid right to the bottom. A kettle of water poured on to it produced a slight thaw, but by the time the steam had gone the bath was solidifying.

I went crunching leaves that had matted and frozen on the lawn all the way to the fence, and poor Pickles, the little black pony, stood stock still on the iron-hard ground beyond, looking petrified. He shook his body in a muscular movement that only horses seem to be able to employ, and tiny globes of frost sprayed round him and fell on the frozen grass. Immediately he began to steam, for the removal of the icy covering released his body heat. He began to trot, as though aware that he must exercise. His feet disturbed more icing from the "cake decoration" in which he had been standing. He is no fool. Like an old soldier he knows how to keep himself comfortable, and "doubles" to keep his circulation going, or so it seems to me.

By one o'clock the scene had changed and for two hours we had a thaw. The trees on the far side of the paddock had turned black and looked wet, but by evening the ground was hardening up again. We had another very cold night, and another thaw today, but this time the melting moment came before noon, and the ponies weren't frosted.

DENIZENS OF THE COUNTRYSIDE

OUR kitchen, sitting-room and dining-room windows here all look out on to the lawn, and this encourages us to birdwatch and note the arrival of different species. The magpies perch in the birch trees, bobbing and swaying in the breeze. Crows hold back and generally stay in the ash and the oak on the hedgeside, while the general traffic is the arrival and departure of starlings, the nuthatch, the great spotted woodpecker, the tribe of finches and the different members of the tit family.

Three days ago, when only the robins remained, a dog fox suddenly walked by. My wife called me and I was fascinated to see the fox go slowly across the lawn like the family dog. He stopped under the large crab-apple tree where I had scattered some rotting apples for the benefit of a flock of hungry mistle thrushes. The thrushes had gone, leaving the remains of the feast, and I was astonished to see the fox pick up and devour an apple. He gulped the half-rotten fruit down and then took another before ambling off to the thicket on the far side of the paddock, whence he departed for our northern boundary to cross the lane. It was exactly a quarter past five and still bright daylight.

The following afternoon at exactly the same time Old Charley appeared again on the lawn and repeated the performance, except that, the apples having been reduced to skin and pips, he scraped here and there for things birds had dropped. The ground was frozen hard and I felt sorry for him. Yesterday when we went down to town I encour-

aged my wife to get some bones from the butcher and some fat for the starving birds. The butcher obliged. We put out a bone shortly before the fox was expected. Had we put it out earlier, a wandering dog might have come for it.

The fox was late. We were sure he was giving us a miss, but then suddenly he was there, sniffing his way about, unearthing things the birds had dropped as they flew off to the hedge and the higher trees. He circuited the birdtables, went away out over the paddock twice and came back again, and then came upwind to the bone. He reminded me of our cat Topsy with a piece of meat when she thinks it may still be hot, for he approached with great suspicion, backed off and circled the bone three times. He left it, and went round the rockery before he trotted in and picked it up. Dropping it, he went in a wide circle again and rushed in to seize the prize and finally hurry away with it.

DENIZENS OF THE COUNTRYSIDE

March 1985

HAVING encouraged the fox to come for titbits on three successive days, I finally went to the butcher and bought a large bag of bones. Old Charley's built-in clock brought him on to the lawn for a fifth and then a sixth day. On the seventh he was accompanied by a vixen, who kept her distance and sat on her haunches while he devoured the prize. He was a most ungallant dog, for he threatened his mate when she moved near, and she went off in a huff, circling the house before appearing on the lawn again to sniff the air. Finally she left, and the dog fox remained to finish gnawing the bone. I was able to watch all this against a background of half-melted snow.

The next day he crossed the lawn at noon and was in no hurry about it. That evening I put out another big bone, but Old Charley seemed a little late showing up. I took my eye off the place where I had left the bone, only to discover that a stray dog had whipped in and stolen the fox's bone. When Old Charley arrived, he followed the scent of the dog for some 30 yards. Meanwhile, I had put out some chicken skin and the fox finally worked up wind and took his supper.

Back to the butcher I went for more bones. The fox was there in the middle of the day again. He returned before dusk to snatch up the biggest bone yet and carry it off down the hedge. Last evening, I was late getting the bone in place, and he was there, waiting. He trotted off but came back again within five minutes to claim his hand-out. He knows when he is on to a good thing.

April 1985

GOATS, I remember my grandfather telling me, weren't allowed to be kept in our part of the world, the Galloway hills having been long overrun by wild goats that cropped the grazings bare, denying the shepherds' flocks much badly needed grass. In Wales there was no such regulation. Goats roamed the hills in Snowdonia, coming down to villages and the gardens of terraced houses to make a nuisance of themselves in winter. Culling goats in Snowdonia was never on. A goat is, after all, the emblem of the Snowdonia National Park.

All this comes to mind with the arrival of a cutting about goats that were a nuisance on San Clemente Island, California. It seems the US Navy planned to shoot the goats until local people became incensed at the plan. In due course the Navy relented. Nets were thrown from helicopters and the goats were shipped to shelters on the mainland. The staff at these centres were beseiged with offers of adoption. At least 1,000 people were interested in the 200 goats removed from the island to reduce damage to plant life. The animals were disposed of in pairs to people with a required minimum acreage of fenced land.

I have been on the brink of goat-keeping for 30 years, but common sense has always prevailed when I have considered my responsibility to look after an animal I take under my wing. Goats may survive in winter without dying from severe cold, but they need to be housed and bedded, fed to supplement their browse at times, and milked.

DENIZENS OF THE COUNTRYSIDE

THOUGH I am often dismayed and horrified by accounts of cruelty to animals, I console myself with the thought that such crimes are at the doors of individuals. The majority of mankind, I hope, displays humanity and concern for animals both domestic and wild.

British Rail spends pounds to make the line safe for badgers. We have road signs telling us to have a care for the hedgehog and the toad, although there are just too many stray cats and dogs for them to merit a warning sign. In Wales they warn

people to beware of sheep, though the Welsh mountain breed generally keeps well away from the road, except in the main street of Blaenau Ffestiniog where sheep have ancient rights.

Our cousins in Australia are no less concerned for their native species, catching up their brushtailed possum, now a nuisance in inner city gardens, and taking it out to the wilderness to prevent it from nibbling away at old trees. They have also gone to great lengths to preserve the mountain pigmy possum, one of Australia's rarest mammals thought to be extinct until it was rediscovered in 1966. At Mount Hotham ski resort in Victoria a ski run and highway divided male from female pigmy possum. The males left the females to their own affairs for most of the year, consorting with them only in the breeding season, but the road and the ski slope effectively prevented the colony expanding, and would, had nothing been done, have led to its extinction.

To provide an overpass was out of the question, so a tunnel was constructed to enable males to visit females without risking life and limb on the road. It cost 34,000 Australian dollars, and the tiny possums used it two weeks after completion, filmed by a remote sensing camera. Victoria is a compassionate state that is saddened by the thought that it no longer has 24 of its native mammals, among them the toolache wallaby, the pig-footed bandicoot (this isn't a term of abuse) and the stick-nest rat. It is thought that, of 700 vertebrates, 191 are threatened.

DENIZENS OF THE COUNTRYSIDE

September 1986

THERE used to be a badger track through the far end of our ground, for Brock would cross the lane and the paddock that lies between to go on down through our jungle. I suppose he went in a wide circle, coming back through another neighbour's fields. I knew he made the trip pretty frequently from his soiling scrapes, and when I had fish offal I used to put it in his track so that he could enjoy a change from the usual items of his diet. All at once the hole in the hedge closed from lack of traffic. It saddened me to think that the badger had been stopped in his tracks, perhaps by a car tearing up the lane late at night. I am fond of badgers. They are comparatively harmless creatures whose only enemies are those who accuse them of being responsible for bovine tuberculosis, and, of course, barbarians who dig them out for badger-baiting.

I remember visiting Phil Drabble and admiring the lengths he had gone to to create setts for badgers that became quite tame and ventured close to his house. A man who was here last week was also a great fan of the badger and had been a badger-watcher all his life. He had actually managed to hand-feed badgers that came out of a sett and ran round his feet, something that delighted him after he had striven to cultivate such trust. It occurred to him, however, that this might have fatal results if the badgers encountered some less benign "badger-watchers" intent upon whisking them away for "sport". This is the problem for anyone who encourages wild creatures. Hand-outs come to be relied upon.

November 1986

THE fox barked, two short yaps and then a period of silence before two more yaps. I lay in bed listening to him. He was out there, on the edge of the lawn, perhaps sending messages to some other fox, or simply listening to his own bark coming back on the echo from the wood.

Down there, on one of his paths through the bramble undergrowth, he stood and barked again. I could hear the echo from the wood myself. Then he crossed the lane and went into the field by the beech wood. He stopped and barked, and the sound was fainter. Ten minutes later, by the luminous clock at my bedside, he was half a mile away, far off and almost out of earshot – yap-yap, and then a long silence. Finally, an even fainter bark. He was gone on his nocturnal journey.

How far would he travel before morning? Six or seven miles by moonlight, I could believe, with rests in which he turned those highly sensitive ears to listen for a reply – a bark like his own, or the unearthly call of a vixen. I had put out crackling from a joint of pork, tightly tied with stout string, and attached to a heavy staple on the birdtable so that it would provide food for the birds. Old Charley had caught the smell and had made a sudden snatch at the prize, breaking string I could never have broken with my hands. There wasn't as much as a bit of crackling on the grass when I went out in the morning. He had probably bolted the lot, string and all, before crossing the lawn and barking.

THE TROUBLESOME MENAGERIE

My feelings about bees were generated a long time ago, as a child. In summer, I would sit close to my grandfather's beehives, watching the endless traffic of bees settling on the flight board and bustling into the hive with their loads of pollen, golden globes fastened to their hind legs.

It was written that I would keep bees. My father kept them and what is in the blood will out. It was the same with bantams. I began with two or three bantams and a dozen, old-before-they-were-young battery hens. Like my bee-keeping the thing got out of hand. I surrounded myself with blue-eyed white muscovy ducks, Khaki Campbells and Aylesburys. My little black araucana hens followed me about crooning because they knew I would feed them another handful of pellets.

The day came when I had to uproot myself and dispose of my hives. I gave my flock of bantams (the dear old brown ladies rescued from the battery all those years ago had lived to a ripe old age) to a man who loved bantams as much as I did. I have come south but am resolved not to venture into husbandry again in a country where the fox is thick on the ground, but I shall always love the cockcrow and the drone of bees in the clover.

July 1970

WHAT skill I have in my hands has never impressed me overmuch, and my lack of manual ability, combined with a sort of ingrowing impatience, results in most of my ventures in carpentry having a falling-away, obtuse appearance. I sometimes have to dispense with the square altogether and pretend that what I am doing is creative and self-expression in wood, rather than to a design. I began on the beehive with all my weaknesses taken out and examined beforehand, and the fact that I wasn't daunted was largely due to my enthusiasm for beekeeping. By some kind of miracle I managed to cut the timber square and construct the whole thing without it ending up with a Tower of Pisa tilt. I painted it, and was delighted when everyone who saw it said that they recognised it for what it had been intended to be, a hive. I had been reserving an alternative description, thinking to call it a sort of dovecote to be hoisted away up on to the top of a pole. But a beehive I had, and when it was roofed and felted, I was elated to find that bees actually came and explored the beehive! I thought to encourage this exploratory traffic of the bees by putting a little wax inside the hive, but I kept that secret to myself and felt very crafty. The visiting bees went in and out all morning despite the smell of the paint I had used the day before.

THE TROUBLESOME MENAGERIE

AFTER lunch I was crossing the court when I stopped and listened. The air was full of bees. I knew the new hive was a good one, but this was something quite beyond comprehension. Had the minister's bees at the far end of the orchard decided to move house? They had. A swarm was on the way. It passed in a slow cloud, like a swarm of locusts, darkening the clear summer sky. I walked at a steady pace after it. It went on past my whiter-than-white beehive, away down the edge of the trees and across my neighbour's land. I followed. My neighbour was having some work done by plasterers who had been stripped to the waist working on the outside of the building. Now they peered out at me from the half-shut windows and asked me if the bees would attack. The bees sailed on, up over the sycamores, and disappeared from my sight. I went slowly back home, remembering long ago summer days when, as a child, I had chased swarms with the rest of the family, banging pots and pans together, or carrying buckets of water, into which grandfather periodically dipped a syringe to squirt water into the air. We always made artificial thunderstorms to bring the bees to rest when there was a swarm. I don't think they ever worked.

I had hardly got back into the house when my wife told me that there had been a telephone call from a friend. Our swarm of bees had just gone into the chimney of the house next door to her. The house was empty. There was a *For Sale* notice outside. I didn't really think that the bees deliberately chose a house that was obviously for sale, but as the lady in question had the key I telephoned the minister and off we went to try to gather the swarm. I had noticed by this time that there wasn't a single bee near my fine new beehive. All that had happened was that scouts of a swarm had been looking for likely quarters. They had rejected my hive. It reeked of paint anyway. The minister and I squirted water at the chimney of the house the bees had chosen, but it made no difference. The bees only went further down. We lit a fire below and tried a little smoke. The bees came out on to the rim of the pot. The hose broke and the water rushed up the sleeve of a kind gentleman who came to hold it, while I stood as high on a stepladder as I could to play a jet on the chimneypot. All was in vain and the bees walked back into the chimney after a while, and settled there. They remained in the flueway for about a week and finally took off for some more comfortable place. But they didn't come back to my new hive.

THE TROUBLESOME MENAGERIE

TAKING bees to the heather is comparatively easy if one has the right design of hive, the box-like units of the type known as National. The older W.B.C. hive, which takes its name from the initials of the man who designed it many years ago, is another matter. It is a series of "lifts" or bottomless boxes resting upon a base, and surrounding the brood box and honey supers, which contain the frames. The very nature of this beehive invites disaster for the man who goes merrily off to the moor without making everything secure. It has to be firmly tied together. It needs to be wrapped in hessian so that bees which escape from the lifts (the hive entrance is, of course, closed by means of little wooden slats which slide into place, or shut off with wire gauze which allows the bees to breathe) are still contained in the general parcel.

Bees on the moor never swarm, I am told. They have too much to do gathering in the great flow of honey to be found when the heather is in full bloom. They do, however, run some risk of becoming slightly disorientated and hanging about on the heather plants for a while. Robbing is a great hazard, a strong colony preferring to take from a weak one, rather than foraging for honey. For this reason most hives are closed down a little, giving the sentries at the door a smaller entrance to guard. Other hazards may be from animals that like to ease their itching hides on bee boxes, or birds that suddenly find that by tapping on the door they can obtain a meal as readily as a boy may get chocolate from a slot machine.

TO prove my steadiness under fire the minister called with the injunction that I must stand by to assist him in cleaning out one of the beehives. He provided me with the traditional panama draped with veiling, and a day or so later, he arrived in more professional garb, gauntlets, wellington boots plus elastic bands, to seal his trouser bottoms from any invading bees that might take exception to our interference with their daily routine. I would keep my hands in my pockets and trust that the bees didn't go up my trouser legs, the minister said. The important thing was to be unafraid. I said quite honestly that I had no fear, but he cautioned me, remarking that it is a natural habit of bees to ascend. Put them in a box and they will explore the upper regions. They do this in the hive. They regard a man's legs as a trapeze artist regards the rope, something to be climbed. What, I asked, must I do when the bees began to find their way up my trouser legs? The minister had a twinkle in his eye. It was quite elementary, he said. Old beekeepers used it. They immediately raised a leg until it pointed upwards and the bees about-faced and climbed back. Confronted by bees making advances up both legs I must get down on my back and stick my feet towards heaven.

At this stage in my limited experience of beekeeping, I must say that I have been unable to confirm that the remedy works. The bees ignored me. I found and identified the queen and drones. I wasn't stung.

THE TROUBLESOME MENAGERIE

MOVING six hives of bees something like 30 miles to the heather is a business not without its hazards. Bees are hard to contain. They need air, and they get furious if they become overheated. They don't thrive on the smell of petrol and all their efforts are directed to escaping. In the meantime, when the hives are on a trailer at the back of a car, one has to keep a constant watch for the load slipping, or some part of the packing being dislodged if the trailer happens to bounce over a boulder on the road up to the moor. It took us three days and we moved two colonies on each day. We did more. We not only moved and established the bees on the site, but we built a fence around it, having brought posts, wire, sledgehammer and crowbar with us in order to do so. None of these things were appreciated by the bees when we let them out. They did their best to rout us, and on one occasion they followed us across the clover field in which we had set them down, apparently determined to drive us into the heather beyond. We retreated so far and sat down to wait patiently for the angry bees to leave, so that we could have our midday meal and return to our labours.

November 1971

MY preparations for the arrival of the pair of golden pheasants were to have been the construction of a roomy run, where they could have cover under branches and somewhere to scrape or dustbath if they do that sort of thing, but I was caught on one foot. The birds arrived and I had nothing done. It was a dark, wet evening, and they, like the ducks, had to have temporary quarters in the old pigeon loft. They were released in the loft. I hardly saw the colour of them, for in the light of the lamp they dashed madly to and fro, and threatened to injure themselves. The next morning, having left them a picking of corn and some water to drink, I had to go away. It was late in the day before I returned. They weren't any more pleased to see me. The hen flew up and perched. The cock dashed to escape by the pigeon trap. I began to see that golden pheasants take a little cultivating. They seem restless, nervous birds.

I went off and looked them up. They have been kept in Britain as aviary birds for 200 years and more. The stock, it seems, isn't improving, and without an introduction of wild blood from China, where they belong, it isn't likely to do so. The bird is small. It relies upon its legs rather than its ability to fly. It has occasionally been cross-bred with one or two other species of ornamental pheasants.

December 1971

ONE thing the golden pheasant cock, with his almost flaxen hair-do, has convinced me of is his restlessness and near instability when compared with his mate. He dashes to and fro endlessly, wearing himself out. He gets almost hysterical when a sparrow, that contrives to find a way into the pen in order to feed, flutters about in the cover I provided for the legitimate tenants. The hen pheasant fluffs her feathers, shuffles down in the bowl of dry earth she has fashioned for herself and casually pecks at seed or larvae. I asked a friend if he thought the presence of a few bantams might help, and he said I might try two or three bantam hens, but certainly not a bantam cockerel, for the golden pheasant is not only a highly-strung, nervous bird, but a somewhat pugnacious fellow and will not tolerate any other cock bird in his pen. Amherst pheasants, I am told, display a similar aggression.

Understandably, this disappoints me. Having a few ducks and the pheasants, and being tied by them, I felt I might as well be hung for a sheep as a lamb and keep a few more, but building yet another pen or run is out of the question, and the golden pheasant cock may go on rushing to and fro like a caged wildcat.

THE TROUBLESOME MENAGERIE

TAKING away the mother muscovy duck from the company of three, and restoring the outcast to his brothers and sisters, has resulted in complete harmony among the ducklings. I take a delight in seeing the youngsters walking abroad in company and rooting in the mowing debris where they seem to find insects or snails and the occasional worm. Ducks have an unselfconscious way of comporting themselves, a dignity that endears them to me. I address them in the mornings when I go to let them out. "Right boys," I say, "first a little water to paddle in, or take a bath, and then you can go where you like." They are locked up for the night on account of the fox. They return to roost at evening and wait for me to fasten the grid behind them. I suppose they would know a fox as an enemy if one came down on the prowl, but they have never seen a fox, or at least they hadn't seen a fox where they formerly lived. For all I know Old Charley may have been down sizing them up, filing away their vital statistics so that he can have one when the time is ripe.

The outcast has now lost his nervousness. His faith in duck-kind has returned. He looks at me a little anxiously, of course, for in the process of saving him from the onslaught of the old duck, and putting him in his own private pen, where he pined and sulked in the dark coop, I man-handled him more than either of us liked. Day by day the memory of his traumatic introduction to this place must be fading. He waddles taller and talks to his companions. The tyrant has gone. I made a present of her to the boy who found and returned the outcast. She won't wilt in isolation. She is a tough old matron, broad in the beam.

This weekend we are off to visit some relatives and the "boys" must stay in prison, but I have arranged for a plentiful supply of water, and more food than ten times as many ducklings could eat, so the foursome will suffer not at all. Their pen is big and airy enough for their needs, and on our return they will once again have the range of the whole orchard. The private pen that housed the outcast duckling is being used now to house the brace of golden pheasants from Liverpool. Kept in the soot and grime of the city the golden ones turned pale and lost condition. I pride myself on being a restorer of out-of-condition birds. In a few weeks, I promise to have a golden gleam on those pheasants.

THE TROUBLESOME MENAGERIE

IT is snowing lightly at the moment, fine snow-flakes that fall like the ash of a garden fire. The sun is shining and there seems little danger of the snow settling or, if it does, covering the grass, but there is something ominous in the silence. The bantams are contemplative. The cocks aren't crowing but conserving their energy and losing no body warmth by fluffing out their feathers. The water troughs were frozen almost solid this morning. When I let the ducks out they flapped round and twitched their tails, shaking off the snowflakes. I had to break the ice for them. They walked after me expecting more than their morning ration of barley and flaked maize. I took pity on them and gave them bread, which I tossed down to them from what used to be the hawk's weathering ground.

Some of the crumbs of bread were over-looked, for when I walked away the ducks followed me again. Ten minutes later a great company of jackdaws, with one or two magpie hangers-on, arrived on the scene and began toddling and hopping to the crumbs. I was amused to see the ducks reacting to this attempted robbery. They flew round the hawk-hut as well as they could with their clipped wings, and came at the daws and magpies from both sides. Muscovies are quite aggressive birds, I am told. Occasionally they will assert themselves over whatever larger fowl shares the park or pond with them. A China goose is considerably larger than a greylag and a small greylag must outweigh the biggest muscovy drake, but the China goose can't stand up to the muscovy and retreats before him.

July 1972

WHEN I was working in the top end of the orchard, cutting grass that screened the bottom of an old pear tree, I became aware of bees passing to and fro to visit an empty beehive. One thing I found early on is that when old hives are inspected, bees somewhere are in a mood to swarm and find new premises. I looked about, discovered some excitement in the colony down at the bottom of the slope, and hurried off to make preparations for taking a swarm should the bees emerge. I came back and camped on the site. Every so often a small number of bees took to the air and went back into the hive. There was no swarming up the front of the hive, but quite a few bees were flying. A brief inspection of other hives had convinced me that the behaviour of those in the bottom corner was abnormal. I knew that, if it didn't rain, I was going to see the swarm emerge. The colony was a large one. They hadn't swarmed last year.

The thing happened quite suddenly. It was like being on the fringe of an exodus from some great public building or a railway terminal. The bees simply poured out. They flowed down the flight board and took wing, but in the confused movement of bees everywhere it was hard to see where they were going. All at once the exodus tailed off. The swarm moved slowly, like a smoke column in the breeze, over the wire fence and into the brambles and thorns that grow around and out of my neighbour's derelict peach house. I waited and saw that the cluster was forming deep in the tangle of old dead limbs of briar. I was determined to take it and hurried off for the smoker, a blanket, a box and some secateurs. The swarm moved into more dense cover as I tried to get at it. In the end, I laid a long branch over the cluster, covered them with the blanket and then, because it was raining steadily, covered this with polythene.

THE TROUBLESOME MENAGERIE

THE book gives figures on the "incubation" of the bee, informing me that the egg hatches in three days. The larva pupates after five and a half days, emerging as a young queen in a further seven and a half days – if the colony needs a queen and the cell was fed royal jelly round about the time the egg was laid. My queenless colony worried me, because it had neither eggs nor brood. After dithering for a precious day or two, I took frames from adjoining hives, each with eggs and brood, trusting to the queenless colony to remedy their own deficiency. They did this with more haste than the expert had led me to expect. There was no queen cell on the two frames of eggs and brood I gave the queenless ones.

I counted the days and looked in at three to see if a queen cell had been started. I was surprised to find that it had been made and completed. It was already sealed. I checked again in five days. The queen had hatched. The colony was active. I actually saw the new queen. She was pale yellow in colour. The book told me that she would be like this for a short time after emerging. My lack of experience, slowness in assessing what was wrong and what needed to be done, has cost the bees perhaps three weeks of increase in numbers and many pounds of honey.

OUT over the house, like a low, slow-moving cloud came the third swarm to emerge from the apiary this summer, a great number of bees progressing happily to pastures new. I watched them with some dismay because it meant that my largest and best colony had split. A swarm of bees in July isn't worth a fly, the rhyme runs. It says nothing about swarms that wait until the middle of August. Nevertheless, I have never been one to take things lying down. I rushed downstairs, put on my shoes and walked as fast as I could – until I was travelling south among my happy bees. They flew over our boundary wall. I had to climb it. They slowly drifted through the upper branches of an ash tree and crossed a gorse clump. I went round it.

They looked down and I looked up. The result was that I fell headlong twice before the migration halted, and they milled round the tip of two very tall ash saplings, where at length they clustered. I judged that something not far short of ten pounds of clustering bees made the tops of those ash branches bend. I went off for a saw, a box and the tools of the swarm-taker's business, but it wasn't for more than 24 hours that the bees came at last into the box and were carried back from whence they had come. In the meantime I had fallen headlong from the ash and badly bruised my shoulders, and frightened the bees with my wildest curses when I slithered time and time again, down the wet grass and the stone scree upon which the ash saplings grow. I hate losing. I cannot bear to be beaten by bees.

THE TROUBLESOME MENAGERIE

AFTER buying 11 bantams last winter, and breeding from them during the summer, I have been taking stock or counting heads. Of the 11, two were cockerels of rosecomb blood, if not perfect examples of the breed. One of the two rosecombs was supposed to be a hen, but a week or two after its arrival, evidently having been a little retarded, it began to crow. One cock crowing is nostalgic music perhaps, but two cocks vieing with each other become a little tedious. I gave one of them away. Now at the counting of heads I find I have no less than 30 birds, with a total of five cockerels, counting the original rosecomb. This means that I managed to breed 20 bantams, 16 hens and four young cockerels. As the old cock crows the young one learns, my grandfather always said. The day is punctuated by the sound of young ones proving that they are applying themselves to the business of learning to crow. I am thinking of getting myself some of those big, sound-insulating ear covers I have occasionally seen technicians wearing. The crowing increases day by day, and day by day I wait to hear from the noise abatement society. I even peer through the hedge when anyone loiters in the lane. It could be one of those fellows with an instrument for measuring sound waves. Soon a letter will come, telling me that I am making a nuisance of myself, adding to the din of traffic down in the town by letting five cocks crow 30 times in half an hour.

There is a remedy, of course. I could pen the cockerels, feed them on barley or wheat and fatten them for the table. Alas, they are true bantams. I doubt very much whether I could improve their size to please the cook. Now that they have the run of the little orchard the cockerels grow bolder. They fly up on to the wall and threaten to come to the back door. They are so proud of themselves that they always pose and throw up their heads and crow. If they can make so much noise before they really have cocks' tails, what will they do when they are fledged, complete with deep wattles and fine hackles? People will consider us a shade eccentric if the family takes to ear shields, but that time is coming. If I write to one of the poultry journals and ask what do I do with a cock that crows all morning they will tell me to wring its neck the night before.

THE TROUBLESOME MENAGERIE

I HAVE been amused to watch a bantam hen who seemed, for a day or two, to think that she was a muscovy duck. Perhaps it came about because the ducks were tolerant of her round their feeding trough while they quickly drove off other hens. The ducks roost by day in a little tight company down near the hedge-bottom. They look contented, serene. The hens bustle about and scrape and scratch endlessly, but this particular little bantam, as well stuffed with barley as any of the ducks since she had made it a habit to ignore the food in the run and race down to join the ducks, would settle down right in the middle of the muscovies.

I suppose muscovy ducks are tolerant creatures most of the time. The bantam followed them, waddling uphill to join in the feast when I scattered pellets for the hens in mid-afternoon, and accompanied the ducks when they waddled away again. At night, she went into the duck shed and roosted there. I was able to check this because the hens are fastened up at night and the ducks are not. The bantam was always out and about with the ducks, who emerge as the spirit moves them, long before I go up to the little orchard in the morning. All at once, however, the bantam went back to the henhouse. Either she had decided that she wasn't a duck after all or perhaps she had isolated herself from the hens and had decided that she had sulked long enough, or the ducks had simply advised her to go back, a duck shed being more squalid than a henhouse.

THE first of the season's bantam pullets have started to lay and I am now able to identify cocks and hens more positively. I was misleading myself and indulging in wishful thinking when I said I had only four cockerels in the 20 or so young that were brought off. I should have used Charles Tunnicliffe's bird-sexing method of dangling a needle over the chicks, noting whether it swung like a pendulum or rotated, although I am inclined to think that in this kind of device the movement may derive from a subconscious analysis of the evidence before the eyes rather than from some mysterious radiation or a preponderance of male or female hormones.

Pullets lay small eggs and genuine bantam pullets lay even smaller ones. One of the dwarfs laid an egg smaller than a pheasant's but improved at the second attempt. Our bantam eggs are much thicker shelled than those of ordinary fowls and, of course, the small birds are generally hardier. They are not as tame but they run for food and outstrip the larger hens by a sort of coot-flight down the orchard, a half-run, half-flying progress amusing to watch. Those that haven't been pinioned arrive airborne and collide with one another, and sometimes with me. Being faster on their feet, they like to take off after the occasional fly that hatches in the dead leaves and takes wing on a mild afternoon. In the summer I noticed young bantams chasing butterflies in the garden and they were often highly successful in the chase. It is surprising how varied the diet of free-range birds is.

February 1973

BEES don't hibernate, but there is a fascinating slowness about them when one takes a quick look under the quilt on a mild afternoon in winter. Here, I tell myself, is something like a slumbering bear. Pounds of bees are down there in a cluster, winged bodies sheltering winged bodies and conserving the warmth. Time is meaningless, an eternity it would seem, marked only by the occasional rising of the temperature by a degree or so. It is irresponsible to knock on the door of the hive to see that the colony hasn't died. One or two slow-moving bees may sometimes be persuaded to come out and investigate, except when it is much colder than the winter sun suggests. I look very rarely. Bees, once they are properly settled down for the winter and have been left enough food, honey or sugar syrup, can be relied upon to look after themselves. They become almost comatose, using little energy and needing to take in very little food to replace what calories they burn.

I make a periodic reconnaissance that sometimes involves just the lifting of the corner of a quilt, although I wouldn't dream of prising off a crown board, or even keeping the roof off the hive for more than a minute. This look round is to make sure that water hasn't somehow managed to seep in, or any roof or lid become slightly displaced to admit damp. A wet colony dies quickly. Some designs of hives, especially if they have been disturbed, allow water to penetrate where the bees' natural sealing has been broken. All my hives are as waterproof as I can make them. All of them, while they are well-ventilated, have an insulation against the cold, rising from hard frozen ground. Bees, like man sleeping out, are better with a "blanket" *under* them.

Yesterday, when I was having a quick look round my own and the minister's bees, which are in the upper part of the garden, I found the ducks waddling at my heels. The bantams, too, must have thought that the hives contained more corn. They not only tagged along but flew up on to the ridges of the hives and waited for me. The bees didn't respond. I didn't see a single one make as much as a quick dash out and then in again. They ignored the vibration of the alighting bantams and the scratching and scrambling around their doors. It was just as well. The bantams are great insect-eaters and will pursue and catch anything that moves, although in summer they seem to leave the bees alone. This is probably because in summer they have plenty of variety, because they have all the excitement they need chasing bluebottles, gnats and butterflies.

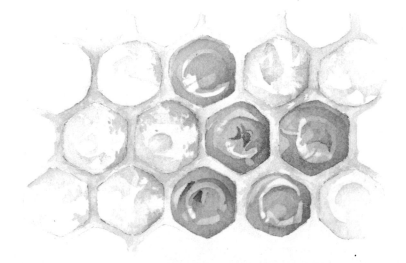

THE TROUBLESOME MENAGERIE

EVERY evening when I went to look at my little bantam hens I would find a fussy, partridge-brown bird who had decided to camp out. I would pick her up and carry her to the henhouse, being scolded all the way for interfering. At the weekend I decided that the time had come to set this bird on a clutch of eggs. She was obviously broody. Camping out had enabled her to get to the barley trough, put out for the muscovies when the hens are penned in. Barley seems to encourage broodiness, probably because it builds up fat and stops the hen laying. I gathered a clutch of eggs and a small coop, and took these, together with a covering cage, to the long greenhouse.

The little hen wasn't long settling down, but that very morning I had to come to a decision about another little black hen. She had decided upon a sit-in, occupying a nestbox, to the indignation of her sisters, 24 hours a day, with only brief departures for food and water. There isn't a cure for broodiness. I set another clutch of eggs in a similar situation in the henhouse itself. The sitting bird has to be penned off, or other hens will lay in the nest should the broody be absent. This has complications and may even bring the whole incubation to nothing. Now I am back on the roundabout. I simply can't resist multiplying the flock. Perhaps I had better put an advertisement in the local newspaper offering bantams for sale. One can only eat so many bantam eggs. Even I have my limit. The other day, I prepared something like 50 bantam eggs to go into the large sweet jar I use for pickling.

FLUCTUATIONS in the weather affect everything that happens in spring, and if spring wasn't late this year it was unpredictable, to say the least, for we had snow when it had no right to be snowing and north winds countering the warmth of bright sunshine, so that the bees went back into the hive and skulked there, their pollen-gathering brought to a stop by bad flying conditions. Pollen-gathering is one of the first things an emerging bee colony does in spring. Every beekeeper knows the stone-hard pollen cells that the bees have filled, as iron rations against the possibility of a lag between the early blossom and the honey flow which comes when fruit and clover, dandelion and charlock are all in abundant bloom.

I hesitated about putting a little honey back in each colony and then decided to let things take their natural course. A softening of conditions within the hive might make the queen lay faster and the brood suffer starvation when it hatched later on. I am not experienced enough to know when to feed. Now, however, when we must be out of the wood, I look into the hives and see that if the bees were short of honey they lost nothing and had quickly stored pollen. The queen is busy. The flight board is warm to the hand at noon when the sun is on it. Honey gatherers drone to and fro, threatening me if I get in their way. Leave us in peace, they say. I am inclined to think that this is half the battle in getting honey in midsummer. Let the bees make the honey. No one else can.

THE TROUBLESOME MENAGERIE

I READ the other day that someone living in Yorkshire claims to have discovered a stock of very docile bees, probably the old English black bee. These, I am sure, were the bees my grandfather had, for his were the best-natured bees I have ever known. The black bee is a legend with beekeepers, most of whom never saw it. So far as the younger generation of beekeepers is concerned it might be a myth, like the golden summers we were supposed to have in the day of the corncrake and the flail. Entomologists can almost certainly produce evidence that there was a black bee native to this country, but until the Yorkshire discovery it was said to be extinct. When it perished I am not sure, but perish it did, and its place was taken by foreigners, bees from Italy, Dutch bees and, of recent years, the Israeli bee, certainly a docile bee but not the hardest working bee in colder regions.

The Italian bees are said to be hot-tempered. I suppose Dutch bees have some national characteristic, real or imagined. Here we talk of the Welsh bee. It isn't a singing bee. It doesn't favour mine shafts or quarry ledges and it doesn't always keep a welcome in the hillsides, but it is a survivor. What is meant is that it is a long-acclimatised species, whether it is Teutonic, Latin or Semitic in origin. If the old English black bee was a docile and manageable species I am inclined to think that this was a characteristic derived from generations of gentle handling. The Victorian beekeeper, like all beekeepers in more leisured times, was in no hurry and handled his bees without excitement.

A LADY who lives on the adjoining estate called by to see if I had any ducklings or even a setting of duck eggs which she might purchase, and I had to tell her that the ducks had long since laid the last egg of the season. I had no ducklings to offer. I was careful not to get more deeply involved in muscovy duck production, I said. In the previous season I had been rather like the old woman who lived in a shoe. Muscovies multiply. A clutch of 18 is not uncommon, and one gentleman in Kirkcudbright had a duck sitting on 27 eggs which resulted in a surviving hatch of no fewer than 24.

While we were talking about ducks and ducklings, I admired the three fine pointers my visitor had brought with her, and she remarked that she was doing well at shows and as a breeder. The production of good stock by enthusiasts is a business far removed from what is called puppy-farming. This is the latest move to meet the demand for "temporary dogs", dogs that delight the sort of people who buy them only as long as they can conveniently be kept. When the pup becomes a burden or a nuisance it is transported to the country and abandoned. This callous practice is being adopted everywhere. The lady with the pointers said she had found two puppies in our lane. They had been "dumped" in a polythene bag. One of them survived and was found a good home.

THE TROUBLESOME MENAGERIE

EVERY day or two I looked into the bottom colony of bees to see what progress they were making. They had been depleted by a prime swarm taking off last summer and had never made good. Now when I began to suspect that the weak and ailing queen was in extremis, if not actually dead, the evidence of diminishing larvae and lack of eggs in the cells convinced me that I must do something to save the stock. I would unite this colony with another one that showed need for improvement. The book said that I could unite by placing a sheet of newspaper between one brood and the other, moving the chosen hive half-way to the one that was being closed down and removing its "furniture". I couldn't do this, however, because of the nature of the ground.

I placed a small hive on the site of the hive being dismantled, united the colonies by the paper method and watched a large number of bees promptly entering the small hive as they returned from foraging. This was quite natural. How were they to know I was manipulating their brood and honey stock, carrying all their young next door? I thought the problem over and decided that I would place the small hive on top of the one I was improving after dark, when all the workers were back. On leaving they would then "home" on the new location. They might even be admitted down below without a battle and a lot of casualties. At night I lifted off the small hive, opened the larger one and tipped the isolationists in. All was peace and harmony the next morning.

A BEE sting is a bee sting and one needs to have the hide of an elephant to ignore the fact. Since the old foul-brood inspector who sold me one of my first colonies had warned me about the danger of taking too many stings (he is himself now gone to tend apiaries in Elysian fields) I look after myself and dress accordingly. The other day, however, spending longer around the hives than a more expert beekeeper might have done, I found that I was not only being molested, but wounded. Bees were inside my veil. How could this happen when I had tied it back and front round my middle and then zipped up my space suit? The answer became apparent when I checked my armour – half a dozen very small holes in the muslin part of the headgear. One's eyes and ears are screened by wire gauze, but if there is a hole in the muslin and a bee can penetrate it, he can work his way to a vulnerable spot and sting. It may seem that a bee requires an entrance hole of about a quarter of an inch in diameter; in fact, a bee can work its way through a surprisingly small hole, using his legs and keeping his wings snug to his body. Beekeepers tend to deny that they ever get stung, because getting stung somehow reflects upon their competence as manipulators of bees. I know how to get fewer stings. It is a matter of visiting the hive at the right time of day on the right kind of day, neither a sultry nor a blustery day, at noon, or on a cool evening.

THE TROUBLESOME MENAGERIE

—————— February 1974 ——————

THERE is nothing I like better than standing watching the ducks. Muscovy and Aylesbury are quite different in temperament. I find the muscovy more intelligent. The Aylesbury is brash and bustling but not as brave as the muscovy. The black and white, pink-billed duck goes through the motions of taking a bath, dipping its bill in the water dish and shaking its rear end to let imaginary water run down its back. The Aylesbury on the other hand pops into the water dish, filling it completely, shuffling around and looking as though it couldn't get out again. Having ruined the drinking water the two Aylesburys toddle off, one behind the other, first downhill and then back up again for no apparent reason. Returning to their point of departure they preen and smooth their heads and necks by a sort of head wobbling that begins at the breast and goes along the flanks. This done, they settle their flight feathers and the small feathers between the wings by stabbing into them and shuffling the bill about.

The muscovies are not prompted to imitate the Aylesburys. They ignore the raucous white ducks and sit sedately looking over the green grass. When they preen they do it more delicately. When they go for a walk they walk sedately and with far less waddling than the Aylesburys. If one decides it wants to be alone it wanders away and stays away, perhaps on the path up beyond the sundial or on the rough slope above the hut. Here the solitary bird will stand in contemplation for an hour or more before returning to the others.

—————— March 1974 ——————

THE one thing I have learned about wintering bees is that they come through best when they have as much of their natural food as the beekeeper can reasonably leave with them. The way a strong colony seals itself up, welding the brood box to the floor of the hive, tacking the crown board down so firmly, and almost hermetically sealing the whole structure within, leaves one in no doubt that they should be left that way. Providing the hive itself is waterproof and reasonably well-made, the bees themselves always cope with excessive ventilation or draughts. Condensation may be a problem if quilts are not of the right material, and any covering like polythene must be shunned.

I look at my hives now. They remind me of seafront boarding houses whose proprietors have gone off to Majorca in the manner of their kind. A knock on the door has a dull echo, but no guardian of the gate comes to see that all is well. The colony is hibernating, using no energy, conserving heat, waiting for time to pass without knowing what time is, I suppose.

There may be something an expert would advise me to do at this stage, but I can think of nothing better than to leave the colonies to themselves. A beekeeper must trust that when the sun warms the flight board there will be a small sign of life, if it is no more than a worker bee popping out and quickly turning round and scuttling back again.

August 1974

MY bantams have the time of their lives on hot days chasing flies, especially after I have been round with a grass-cutter. They are remarkably fast on their legs and adept at twisting and turning after a bluebottle or a gnat. I am always fascinated to watch them at the business. Insects form a good part of their diet I think. They love to forage for larvae under the dead grass on damp days and go fly-catching when the larvae hatch on hot days. I am amused to see how the two little hens who hatched duck eggs have taught the ducklings the fly-catching business. The ducklings are much closer to the ground than their foster mothers but they have acquired great agility and while the bantam hens rush off after elusive bluebottles, the ducklings run here and there in pursuit of lesser flies.

The beehives, surely a great source of food for insectivorous birds, are completely avoided. Neither the bantams nor the innocent ducklings venture to feed on bees, although blue tits occasionally loiter near the hives. I am inclined to think that they wait for the aged worker *in extremis*, or swoop down to take a corpse bundled out of the hive by the cleaners who take care of such things and tip bodies over the flight board in the course of their daily work. I notice that the bigger hens make forays after insects too, but like bigger fish, they need a bigger lure. A cabbage butterfly is chased until the old ladies positively rock on their legs, sometimes catching the titbit, but more often than not having to watch it sail over the hedge, oblivious to the danger it was facing.

THE TROUBLESOME MENAGERIE

WITH the first of the honey harvest in the ripener (a large cylinder with a spigot or tap which enables honey to be drawn off after the air bubbles have risen through it and the honey is settled and ripened) I begin to appreciate the fruits of my labour. Nothing tastes quite so good as the first honey of a new season. Honey will keep, but it crystallises in time. Although it may be made to flow again by standing the jar in warm water, it never tastes quite so good as the honey that ran into that jar on a warm summer's day. I have taken back to the hives all the cappings – the wax "seal" which has to be sliced from the frames in order to extract the honey – and the residue of mixed wax and honey left in the extractor. The bees get to work and store the salvaged honey in the frames also returned to them.

Now I await the slower honey flow of late summer which I may or may not take from the colonies. We don't use a pound of honey a week, even when honey cake is made and I have an occasional egg-milk-and-honey drink. I feel that leaving the bees short is a foolish thing to do. Any colony left well-stocked will produce a good harvest early in the following season. Those left with a poor reserve breed up slower and have a harder job to take advantage of the supply available once the real honey flow arrives. I have given up taking bees to the heather because of the difficulty of extracting such heavy honey, to say nothing of the labour involved in transporting hives. My bees produce as much honey here as they did when they were allowed to get the first honey flow and were moved to the moor to work on the heather. I was thinking about the way I use my bees the other day when the postman arrived with a letter from America accompanied by a cutting from the *Arkansas Gazette*. The news item mentioned the dwindling of the wild honeybee in that State. The wild bee's decline this year threatened the apple crop in Arkansas. To compensate for the dearth of wild bees, 600 hives were moved to ensure the pollination of 300 acres of apple trees in one part of north-west Arkansas alone. Rent-a-hive may yet become more lucrative than honey production. Beekeepers have been renting out hives at five dollars each, but the price is almost certain to rise. Melon growers are in a similar plight to the apple grower, but the continual movement of bee colonies reduces honey yield drastically.

One ominous fact lies behind the decline of pollinating insects, however, and that arises from the continued use of insecticides and dangerous sprays. Renting out hives may be a business proposition, but bees will have to be insured against loss. In addition to this is a danger of starvation if the honey stocks aren't maintained.

THE TROUBLESOME MENAGERIE

THE old battery hens like apples, and I hardly picked a single windfall this year, for they and the muscovies made short work of whatever fruit fell from the trees. Not only do the old dears like apples, they know a dessert apple from a cooker. They have a sweet tooth, and when I was picking some well-ripened Laxtons and Golden Delicious, I dared not drop one or the hens joined me in the rush to get it. They seemed oblivious to the fact that I was *gathering* apples. They weren't in the least put off by my shouting and trying to frighten them.

Ducks are not quite so brazen as hens. They defer a little to me as master of the yard, and will slow up and allow me to pick up whatever I have dropped, but the hens have no fear. I suppose this is because they were raised in pens and have far less fear of man. I find the bantams more flappable and nervous. I have only to look at them and they become uncomfortable and begin to walk away. The matronly battery birds look me in the eye. "Don't be silly," they seem to say, "the apple grew on the tree. It is no more yours than ours. It rolled down the slope and we saw it first!" They haven't been laying because of the protracted moult. I tell them firmly that it really isn't good enough and there will have to be an alteration, but here again they look intently at me and I am the one who is disconcerted.

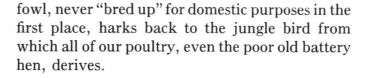

March 1975

AFTER I had managed to identify the bantam cockerels as Araucanas, thanks to a gentleman who sent me Dr J. Baty's *Bantams and Miniature Fowl* by W. H. Silk, a lady whose Araucanas were illustrated in the book wrote to give me a little of the history of the breed. The Araucana is a singularly attractive little fowl with a small comb, a feather crest and what the book calls "ear muffs". It is bred in a variety of colours. Mine are what might be called black and brown-red and they shine as though lit by the setting sun. I had no idea that they are comparatively scarce and that the breed was bantamised about 45 years ago. Bantamised bantams are birds bred down by selection, while I suppose the dwarf fowl, never "bred up" for domestic purposes in the first place, harks back to the jungle bird from which all of our poultry, even the poor old battery hen, derives.

"The Lavendar Araucana bantams have an interesting history," says my correspondent. "A Mr George Malcolm who lived in East Lothian in the 1930s decided to bantamise the breed and after this concentrated on the Lavendar or Grey Araucana. He used the crested Lebar, an autosexing breed obtained from Cambridge University, and bred from an inbred line of White Leghorns crossed with some Araucanas recently imported from Chile. Later Mr Malcolm used a very small, laying-trial winner Leghorn to improve the laying qualities. We lived in East Lothian and were lucky enough to be given some of these Lavendar Araucanas after seeing them at the Royal Highland Show. Our present stock descends in part from them. Mr Malcolm no longer keeps any fowl but is secretary of the Belted Galloway Society.

"Until 1973 there hadn't been a breed standard for Araucanas. I, along with others, wrote one and had it accepted by the Poultry Club. Since then the breed has been shown increasingly. However, the British Araucanas are very different from those in Holland, Germany and North America. There they tend to be tail-less and are adorned with tufts of feathers growing out from either side of the head. This is unique to the breed and is not in the least like the beard and muffling of our birds."

FOR about a week I have been fascinated by the behaviour of a wild cock pheasant who comes to the pen in which my own, home-bred cock pheasant lives with his harem of bantam hens. Both birds are in excellent condition and I think claim the territory as far as they are able to do so, considering that the penned bird can't drive off his rival and the rival can't take over the pen. They shape up to one another from very early morning onwards, the wild bird crouching and threatening and pecking at his rival behind the wire, and the tame bird doing likewise. I put down a trap and caught up the wild bird to take a close look at him and make sure he couldn't be the cock who escaped from prison a few months ago, and whose departure wasn't really lamented. The caged pair had taken to battering each other and handing out bloody heads almost every other day. The wild bird is not the former occupant of the pen, but he could easily end up inside if he persists and I can find some way of keeping the rivals apart. I let him go, however, and he wasn't too terrified after his brief confinement in the trap. He was back that same day, running up and down and posing head-on with his rival until he looked like his reflection in a mirror, which he might have been but for the fact that the penned bird has a white ring on his neck.

Every day when the wild bird isn't on hand, the penned bird crows and flaps his wings and the wild bird soon arrives on the scene. After a period of confrontation the wild bird drifts off into the orchard, but I have seen him made to turn round and come back by the penned cock lifting his head and making that *cok-cok* sound pheasants use to contact one another. When I go out, the wild bird takes wing, but he goes no distance. He flies almost vertically and drops down on the other side of the wall. If I walk round there he stalks along, but not too warily, and picks seeds or insects as he goes. He is all but tame. The behaviour of the aggressive little bantam cocks destroys a poaching legend. They crow, but show no inclination to fight the cock pheasant. The wild cock pheasant ignores them completely if they stroll past while he is challenging the penned bird. It is as though the domestic birds and the wild pheasant completely fail to recognise not just a remote kinship, but the fact that they are all fowl. The old poachers were said to release a fighting cock to draw a cock pheasant to them. The fighting cock would soon dispose of the long tail. Well, no bantams fight more readily than my eight little fellows, but not with the wild cock pheasant. I begin to think that even a gamecock would fail to raise his hackles to a cock pheasant.

THE TROUBLESOME MENAGERIE

NO one can keep livestock of any kind without a certain wear and tear, an erosion of the soil, a breaking up of paths, a degree of delapidation that outpaces maintenance. When I had sheep I became aware of gaps in hedges and holes in fences and new paths along the slope in both orchards, as well as new ways up the cliff where the sheep bundled their way along, regardless of thorns and brambles. Human beings make their own trails and paths and create their own kind of wear and tear, but woolly creatures like sheep and long-coated dogs can drive through thorns with impunity. Hens may not be able to bark trees the way hungry sheep do, but they flap up to pick succulent foliage and sweet young buds and florets. Much worse than this, however, they dustbathe and puddle their way along to break up what seemed well-trodden, stony paths and create screes. I must say that it delights me to come upon an old hen having the time of her life dustbathing. I even see a certain dreamy abandon about the

dust-bathing bird. They sometimes can't get deep enough in the light soil as they fluff their feathers and lie with one wing outstretched, basking in the sun. They move on, however, finding better holes, and leaving places strewn with feathers and fragments of dead grass.

I come along with the barrow or the two-wheeled truck and find my progress abruptly halted because a wheel has dropped into one of the dust-baths. This kind of thing must stop, I say, and go off to find a shovel and a rake to make good the damage. The hens seem to take a delight in getting even. In two or three days they have worked their way through my hardcore of stone rubble and regained their "spa". I give up and let them scratch and sunbathe, and wonder where it will all end. Stones that are scratched off the path are trundled on down the slope. There they get in the cutters of the mowing machines and do a lot of damage to it. I have to rake before I can cut, or cut high and let the growing grass accumulate more debris from the hens' scratching higher up.

It is all picturesque in a way, I suppose. Hens on a smooth green lawn would look unnatural. Hens that never fluffed up in a dustbath wouldn't look healthy. Ducks always bore into tussocks to get at snails and worms, and they paddle the ground round the water troughs. A garden is a garden and free-range means what it says. I look at the mutilated fruit trees and the scars remind me of the sheep I once had. One day I will probably look at a depression in the path and think of my hens.

THE TROUBLESOME MENAGERIE

——— *May 1975* ———

THE comedian of my collection of ducks is a dark brown to black one, dumpier and fatter than the rest. She goes faster than the others, has much more to say and is in and out of everything, here, there and everywhere, it seems. She looks at me with a quizzical expression as she hurries past. I get the feeling that she is afraid I may pounce on her at any minute. A few weeks ago she was suddenly missing. I searched the hut, the duck shed, every place I could think of. Could the fox have come down and taken such a fast, voluble, garrulous duck without alarm? I couldn't believe it, but it seemed to have happened.

I was put down, depressed, and wandered up the path by the sundial, disconsolate at the loss I had suffered, when I suddenly met her coming out from a tangle of thorn screened by thick ivy. She had plenty to say as she went bumping and waddling down to join her sisters. I poked in the thorns and then went and got the secateurs to cut my way in. There had been four eggs in the hut each morning for several days instead of the expected five. Old dumpy had taken to laying away. She had five eggs in a private nest up in the thorns. I lifted them and gave her a pot egg to encourage her. She was talking a lot the next morning when I encountered her, but she hadn't laid an egg to keep the pot egg company. I think she was saying I seemed to take her for some kind of fool who didn't know a pot egg when she saw one.

——— *July 1975* ———

MY enthusiasm for the bees gets stronger as I find my manipulation of colonies working. Now I call my group of hives – seven is the perfect number, but I have eight – an apiary. I am not sure whether such a small set-up qualifies for such a pretentious description, but making an apiary has meant siting each hive on a level base, a flagstone set in the slope, and making sure that the entrance to the hive faces the morning sun. In each case I was careful not to move the hives, and this meant working in range of the angry bees, who did not appreciate my efforts on their behalf with trowel, shovel, grass shears and so on. I was, of course, well protected in the vital areas, but since the weather was warm (it is best to work around beehives in warm weather when the main strength of the colony is away gathering food) I did not feel like putting on my overall suit. This proved a mistake. The odd defender of the gate came out and buzzed me. Finally I was attacked. I was staggered to discover that my trousers were not sting-proof. They are lightweight material. The bees quite literally caught me bending. I have been stung in many places in my short experience of beekeeping, but never on my latter end.

Despite the attacks I carried on and finished the work. Now everything is in order I await the fruits of my labour and imagine that the greater part of it will come next year. There will be no swarms and perhaps not as much honey as last year, although my stronger colonies are doing very well and the four new ones created early in May are thriving.

THE TROUBLESOME MENAGERIE

A HEN blackbird, a handsome bird with a sooty, brown-mottled breast has begun to follow me about, and I find myself talking to the bird while she cocks her head and appears to be listening. I am not sure what kind of noises one should make to a blackbird. I huff and puff to the muscovy drakes, and they huff and puff back, or make that noise that sounds like huffing. The drakes seem pleased with my response. I bleep to the muscovy ducks because they bleep at me. The ordinary ducks quack incessantly. If I imitate their noise they fall silent and cock their heads and make me feel a little self-conscious. I have a feeling they think I have gone mad, but the old battery hens talk back. I don't know what I am saying to them, but they seem to understand the language and encourage me to say more. I wish I knew what we are on about. It would take a Lorenz to interpret, but I do feel that communication is close.

It is frustrating not to be able to break through. Mind you, it could become a nuisance if at feeding time one had to take up all the quibbles and complaints of 50 hens and a dozen ducks, as well as the squabbles of the cockerels. I am content to let it remain one-sided for the time being. The old cock pheasant in the pen encourages me to talk. He would be a regular gossip now that he has become so tame. I think he or one of the muscovy drakes might be worth knowing. The gentle female blackbird has nothing to say, but I feel that one of these days she will feed from my hand, like the robin who rewards me every so often by singing a song to me after he has eaten.

THE splendour of autumn is not always so much the change in the colour of the leaves, so far as I am concerned, but the transformation I see in the plumage of the muscovy ducks. From early spring, without a pond or any large quantity of water in which they might bathe, my poor ducks tend to be a slightly muddy colour as a result of their amours. I look at them and wonder if they really care about being resplendent drakes and well-set-up ducks, for they might at least bathe in the troughs. Instead, they behave like schoolboys, shake a minimum of water over themselves and quickly preen without bothering about their final appearance. By the end of the summer the ducks, in particular, look pretty well worn-out and very shabby as a result of their determination to lay away and go broody whatever happens.

One solution to the problem would be not to trim the flights of the birds, and simply let them fly away to pastures green and deep weedy waters, in which they could have the time of their lives, but someone might shoot them. They are very tame, naïve birds and a fox or a dog could easily slink up and kill them, one by one. All this forces me to be content with the six-month eclipse, and it is well worth waiting to see the change in autumn, for after the moult the muscovies are magnificent. Their white is whiter than white and their blue becomes iridescent and almost green. The red on the heads of the drakes matches the ripe rowanberry and outdoes the hawthorn, and I am proud of them.

THE TROUBLESOME MENAGERIE

December 1975

THE weather affects us all. For a long time I have observed how my hens and ducks react to change. When there is a touch of frost they are ravenously hungry in the morning. Wet weather drives the matronly old hens to the shelter of the bushes and finally into the henhouse. The ducks are not all as fond of the rain as one might expect. The farmyard breed get their heads down and never stop, but walk on, boring into the roots of the long grass to find worms, snails and other titbits. The muscovies forage far less. They stand about as though waiting for something and often look quite disconsolate. They make take-off runs in a gale. The farmyard ducks stretch themselves on their legs and fan the air with their wings as though they know their flying muscles have long since atrophied.

Today we had a gale and I have to confess that I went up to let the birds out much later than usual. The old hens were reluctant to come out. The very late bantam chicks, still not much bigger than my clenched fist, were out and about immediately, getting under my feet and sometimes almost getting blown off their own. A black bantam hen that has a great sense of responsibility and wouldn't wait for her share of the pellets made a beeline for her laying place in the small shed along the path. The thirsty ducks trundled down for a drink, pushed off course by the force of the gale, but getting there because they are streamlined. Half an hour later there was hardly a bantam or a battery hen to be seen.

March 1976

MORE than a sprinkling of fine hail fell upon me as I went up to the hens this morning. Winter has taken over, even though the daffodil buds are nine inches high and snowdrops are everywhere. I am inclined to be sorry for the fowl in these conditions. The water trough freezes, the mud congeals and then becomes iron-hard. A cold wind sweeps across the grass, freezing granules of hail to the stalks.

A duck, on the other hand, has two good things about it – a considerable thickness of very fine down and small feathers, and a good layer of body fat. The hen with fat, too, fluffs up the coat she wears until it forms an insulating barrier between the inner warmth of her body and the cold beyond her elevated feathers. Hens avoid moving too much in cold weather, so retaining heat and also using fewer calories. At roost they wait for it all to end, without a human's ability to assess the passing of time or the drawback of imagination.

THE TROUBLESOME MENAGERIE

WITH the passing of time I have forgotten exactly when I brought the 12 hens from the battery, but I know they are at least six years old and have survived much longer in my hands than they would have done if the battery keeper had had his way. I must admit that by keeping them on as pensioners I have let them grow tough. They have consumed a lot of food without ever going back to the 300 plus eggs a year. A hundred people have been deprived of chicken in the basket and I have wallowed in sentimental self-indulgence. Every so often there have been casualties. A hen that works so hard in her first year of life cannot go on forever. My 12 birds have come down to seven. I have buried five, each one mourned a little because she was a pet, but to be quite truthful I have always felt that the friendliness of the old battery hens was cultivated in that formative year in the cage. None of my free-range, wild-bred birds was ever as trusting as the old, brown battery birds. The latest one to go died yesterday. When I let the birds out in the morning this particular old dear showed no interest. I lifted her down into the yard, but she would not eat. In the afternoon she was tucked into a nestbox and I could tell that she had died even before I touched her. I went off and dug a deep grave for her.

Now we are seven. I could not make an end of any of them. I have promised them a home until they are finished with living, and then perhaps I may cut down the bantam flock and let the muscovies fly out when their flight feathers grow. Pity is a powerful emotion but I am not ashamed of it. An economist would have no time for what I am doing. He would say that it is irrational to keep old hens when they no longer lay more than a few eggs a year. I am delighted not to be of his religion. Facts and figures cannot really give him as much satisfaction as I get from seeing those bundly old hens running to meet me at feeding time.

April 1976

BY the middle of the last summer I was the proud possessor of 11 sound, solid bee-hives – the apiary I had always promised myself – although I must admit that with one step forward and two steps back my colonies numbered six at the close-down of the season. They had been up to seven but I re-united one with another to bring them through the winter. This left me with five highly desirable properties untenanted and freehold to be offered to the first applicants in 1976. The six colonies came through the winter without mishap. Three of them had honey in the super when I looked in on them in February. I make a habit of taking what honey I can early in the season so that the bees can work for themselves for as long as possible.

Now I plan to expand my colonies by splitting broods inside the hive and separating them in due course. I should be able to do this with four of my six and, with any luck, have ten good stocks at the end of the season. I smile now when I think of the way I began and how I chased my swarms and took a pride in recapturing them when, if I had known what I was about, they need never have swarmed at all. If I had concentrated on the proper management of my colonies they would never have left or even made preparations for leaving. Early in the season I plan to set about dividing colonies. This will be about the last week in April, if the weather is right. In the meantime, apart from the spring clean, I shall leave the bees to their own devices – the pollen gatherers gathering pollen, the carriers of water doing their job.

THE TROUBLESOME MENAGERIE

WHILE I am no Lorenz I have come to learn something about ducks and other waterfowl, and in recent years ten particular ducks. Anyone who keeps a pet duck discovers that it has a character and personality of its own. It is not just a long-necked, watertight bird that enjoys the rain. It is far more intelligent than a hen, for instance, and it is capable of displaying what seems to be affection for its owner. Ten ducks cannot be turned into pets. They remain a duck group or groups of ducks, and the shyness, wariness or nervousness of one particular bird tends to inhibit the rest somewhat. Separate the individuals and you may discover their character.

My ten birds comprise seven muscovies and three mixed-breed, farmyard ducks. The muscovies don't associate with the farmyard strain who are talkative, flappable, busy and prone to erratic hurrying from one place to another. The muscovies sit with all the dignity of monumental lions, enjoying the sun and the softness of the close-cut, green grass. I am courted by two of the muscovy ducks. They look up at me appealingly, blue-eyed and beautiful, knowing I will turn back to give them just a small handful of food in addition to their daily ration. They talk about me when I have taken myself off, making the "tweedling" sound that muscovy ducks make in the laying season.

The old drakes, who really should be called ganders because they are so big and crusty, make no sound at all. They have a phlegmatic outlook, and when I use the rough grass-cutter they sit still and keep their cool until I almost cut round them, although they always rise at the last moment and make an unhurried departure. We get on very well, especially at locking-up time, when, if the drakes are out, I simply point to the door of the shed and they toddle off and go in for the night.

The farmyard ducks are clamorous and would-be stop-outs, but when I come up the path they make an undignified scramble to go in. I come to close the door, and their conversation increases in volume as though the fox had come after them. I lock them up and they fall silent. First thing in the morning they each lay an egg, and when I open the door they are first out, talking nineteen to the dozen, flapping their wings and wafting feathers and debris about for all they are worth. The dumpy one without a tail, who is almost certainly descended from a Cayuga, bundles off round the corner to the place where I scatter the food for my mixed collection of hens and ducks. Less intelligent birds troop after me, but the ducks go where they know the food will be scattered and wait there. I could write a book about them.

October 1976

MY reputation as a charmer of bees (depending entirely on luck!) spreads in my part of the world as a result of the capture of two swarms, neither of which came from my own colonies. I took the first swarm after I noticed a nucleus box being scouted by visitors and decided that the swarm would arrive the following day. It did, and it housed itself without any help from me. I was telling a friend about this five days later and drew his attention to the signs of a second swarm about to take place.

This swarm, I pointed out, would be light-coloured Italians. I expected them to arrive at the box the following day sometime between 12 and 2 o'clock – the time nearly all the swarms I have handled seem to arrive on the scene. It was just past noon when I mentioned the fact. My friend gaped when the swarm arrived – a day early, but housing itself unaided. I could not resist saying that my great-great grandmother was a witch and that I proposed to set up in business as a swarm-taker. Two swarms housing themselves in a week and both prime swarms is something remarkable. Now both are working at full blast and putting honey in the super. I am reluctant to predict a third.

WHEN I go to shut up the birds against the fox, who has twice managed to get there before me, I sometimes wonder what an unseen observer would make of it. One elderly brown hen has a habit of being last in. Every other bantam and hen will be dozing at roost. The farmyard ducks will be under cover, but this old hen will be standing there like an old lady in the street after the last shop has closed. I walk her in, shepherding her along and talking to her. I sometimes think she stays out late to get this little bit of attention. She clucks and croons and ambles ahead, rocking a little on her old legs, and finally going up the ramp and into the henhouse to be greeted drowsily by one or two of her sisters.

The muscovies wait on the slope of the little orchard, their heads up and looking alert. They know what they must do. I do not speak to them. They are shepherded in total silence. They hurry if I speak and their crests are inclined to rise, so I keep mum, and simply hold out my arms. One by one they waddle to the hut, flap up over the board that serves as a doorstep, and go in. I shut and fasten the grill, and depart, but sometimes they immediately have a squabble among themselves. I walk back and bang on the sides of the hut, which brings them to order, at least until I am out of earshot. Anyone watching would surely conclude that I am, to say the least, a little eccentric.

THE TROUBLESOME MENAGERIE

FOR the first time I allowed the muscovies to carry on after the moult without chopping the primary feathers, with the result that they emerge from the hut each morning for a flight down the slope. They are, however, getting on in years a little now, and their muscles need training before they can really become airborne. Their confidence, too, is lacking, and as one comes to the gate of the hut it will hesitate, blocking the path of the bird behind while it plucks up courage to fly.

I go on to the path above and scatter food and the first bird to make a flight, and then come uphill, begins to gobble it down. The last one gets very little breakfast, but it is always a last but one who stands there longest, thinking about this unnatural business of flying. I slip up to the side of the hut and frighten the poor bird into flying, but it is rather like making a small boy jump into a swimming pool. A duck may take to water easily but when it has been earth-bound for a year or two it isn't at once in its element when forced to fly. My nervous muscovies have to work at take-offs and landings first and learn the principles of flight as they go along. The farmyard ducks have no such problems. They could not take off and fly even if I pushed them.

A READER who lives in Botswana writes to me about a note I wrote some time ago concerning my duck who lived in the henhouse and apparently regarded itself as a hen. "When we were living in Marandella about two years ago," my correspondent remarks, "we were breeding turkeys and slipped some duck eggs under one of the turkeys. She eventually hatched ten turkey chicks and two ducklings. She mothered them all impartially, and the two ducklings thought they were turkeys, and ran around quite happily with the flock, though they sometimes found it hard to keep up, when they called loudly, and the mother would go back and hurry them along. The funniest episode was when they discovered the dam – they took to the water immediately, with the mother turkey frantically running along the bank, with all the small turkeys after her, all screeching at the tops of their voices.

"Every day after that, when the ducklings took to the water, mother patrolled the bank, calling at intervals, seeming to accept that there was a difference, but still accepting responsibility for them. If our dogs went anywhere near either the turkey chicks or the ducklings, they were severely pecked by Mum for their pains, as were human strangers. Even when the ducklings became ducks, and stayed on the water with the other ducks, if that particular turkey was at the water's edge, they would greet her, and she them. It all really points to Konrad Lorenz's theory that 'imprinting at birth' is the key, and if we upset the normal course of things, then we can expect the abnormal."

THE TROUBLESOME MENAGERIE

THE telephone ringing downstairs disturbs me when I am at my desk, and sometimes, I must admit, I tend to let it ring, hoping that someone else will answer it, although it is just as irksome to be called down with the reproach that the call was for me. The call is always for me when the hens begin cackling. My imagination gets to work. I see the fox slinking forward on his belly to make off with one of my birds, as he has done before this, or the crow bullying his way among the flock to make off with a small chick. The tawny owl looms in my nightmare along with magpies and jays. Hens don't cackle for nothing, I tell myself, forgetting that they do cackle for next to nothing on most occasions.

It was an incessant cackling that drew me up to the little orchard one afternoon ten days back, and I stood there looking across the grass to discover what the indignant, head-high sounding-off on the part of the near hysterical hens was all about. It was some minutes before I spotted it, a small thing indeed to be responsible for such a bedlam of cackle. A half-grown kestrel sat in the open looking large-eyed and alarmed by the fuss he had caused. I walked towards him, expecting him to fly away with the speed a small falcon can summon, but he didn't. He was not able to fly. At about the time I heard voices beyond our far wall and felt sure I was under observation. I called and asked the unseen youths if they had lost something, for it now seemed that they had captured this newly-fledged kestrel and lost it again, but they muttered something about minding their own business or my minding mine. I heard them go down to the corner and over the stile which brought them on to the footpath running alongside our lowered boundary. They hung about there for a while but finally went off.

I got my seatrout net and caught the falcon to examine it. It seemed to have little strength but it was strangely hand-tame, and the whole thing, as I imagined it, filled me with indignation. I become furious at the thought of this kind of wanton behaviour. I took the little kestrel to the hut and left it there while I went to see if Topsy the cat had anything to offer. By chance she had brought down a shrew. I commandeered her kill and took it to the kestrel, who devoured it greedily. It seemed to me that if I supplemented this first meal with a little raw meat I would be able to set the bird free next day. The meat went down well and Topsy was later robbed of a young blackbird to give the kestrel something to pellet, but when I attempted to release the kestrel he had to be shaken from my hand. He didn't fly but hopped like a jackdaw. I had to catch him again and give him another day's convalescence.

The following day I tried again but he just didn't manage any sort of flight, although he has improved in condition with every meal. I have made two further attempts to encourage him to depart but he just won't make the effort. Until he comes to it I am saddled with him. I fear that if I just leave him to his fate he may be killed by a cat or caught by boys.

THE TROUBLESOME MENAGERIE

EACH day the little kestrel seemed a little stronger and better able to flit to the other end of the hut. I fed him little strips of best beef and the odd shrew which Topsy left. After a whole fortnight of convalescence, the bird's eye brightened. He looked about in the distance-measuring way of his kind, and I hoped that one morning he might actually flit past my head and win his freedom, but he didn't. What he did was look for a juicy bit of meat for his breakfast. The final stage of his convalescence had to be faced. If he didn't fly like a falcon I would have to persevere and teach him his business. I fed him at seven in the morning, and after he had ruffed up and preened I pushed my finger against his breastbone and asked him was he ready to go. He bobbed once or twice as we went through the door of the hut and cocked his head, looking up at the sky, as though deciding that it was a great day for it.

There is no way in which a falconer reads the eye of the bird, for the eye of a kestrel is black. Unlike the eye of the hawk, the pupil's dilation and contraction isn't visible. All at once the little kestrel was off. He flew as swiftly as any sparrowhawk and swept round to perch in the walnut tree. An hour later I watched him preening himself in the sunlight, looking over his back as he raked his feathers with his hooked beak. Then he was away in the blinking of an eye. Nothing could have pleased me more. I decided long ago that keeping any bird of prey captive, by any means whatsoever, is a crime. There is no way the thing can be justified, licensed or unlicensed.

THE very old brown hens go off the lay one after another, and perhaps for good, for they have done more than their stint at egg production. I couldn't blame them if they never laid another egg. The odd one still does her best however, and what intrigues me is that when they were all much younger, these well-bred birds would always lay in the nestbox. Now things are different and the well-trained old biddies are kicking over the traces and laying away. The jungle habit returns to them in their declining years. They behave like wild birds, not only in their laying-away, but in the way they go about it. I have watched them and they always do their best to slip off unobserved. Bantams do this of course, but bantams are nearer to the jungle and the forest floor than these sometime-battery matrons whose blood lines have been controlled by scientists to make them conform to a very exacting pattern of behaviour.

The old brown hen walks a few paces, looks about, steps into the long grass, stretches her neck and looks above the grass like an ostrich, catches sight of me keeping an eye on her, and goes no further until I look elsewhere. I step round the corner of the hut and wait there for a moment or two. The old brown hen listens and takes another pace into the jungle, but she pops her head up the moment I pop mine round the corner of the hut to see where she has gone. After a while, having decided where the nest must be, I take myself off. Later on I find the nest and pick up all the eggs.

THE TROUBLESOME MENAGERIE

THE old brown hen has gone broody each summer ever since I rescued her from the battery, so long ago now that I cannot remember when it was. All I can say is that she, and her surviving sisters, are old ladies now. One thing about such amply proportioned birds is that they are ideal for brooding chicks. They make wonderful mothers. Not all of the old battery birds go broody, however, and this particular bird seemed to me to deserve to be given something more to do than simply sitting it out, morbidly looking at the dull furniture of the deserted hen-house. I gave her a few eggs to sit and wasn't very concerned whether she brought off chicks or not. The hatch was two. I moved the old bird and her chicks to a small hut at the other end of the orchard.

It seemed likely that with such big feet and two tiny bantam chicks so quickly lost in the vast covering of feathers, the old bird would be bereaved of her entire family in a short time. I was wrong, however. The chicks somehow managed to avoid being trodden to death and they were well looked after by their enormous mother. She scratched for them and taught them what to pick and what to avoid. She fluffed up and her hackles rose when she thought they were threatened. What was more, she brought them to their adolescence without walking off and leaving them, which is the normal behaviour of most birds when their offspring reach a certain age. Pullets fend for themselves at about ten weeks and the mother bird no longer recognises any maternal tie, but the old brown hen was different. She fussed round her brood of two after they were fully fledged.

They stayed with her until at last she took them along to the old henhouse where she rejoined her sisters. One of the two youngsters didn't quite grasp what had happened, but the other went up to perch, leaving a rather bewildered brother crouched under a gooseberry-bush canopy, in which hens often seek shade from the sun. I saw this bird by chance when I went to lock up for the night and flushed him out of cover, clapping my hands to get him on the run. He gathered his wits, remembered where his foster mother had gone, and ran into the henhouse. The old brown hen clucked scoldingly at him as he entered. I was relieved when this stop-out perched the following evening. The fox always picks off birds that remain out. Amalgamating family groups is generally beyond the person who keeps hens, for these groups form by a natural process. One discovers who belongs to whom by watching birds after they have emerged from the henhouse in the morning. There is always a problem when an entire goup refuses to roost with the rest, and more than once I have failed to keep bantams under one roof.

November 1977

A FRIEND came to see me this week bringing a cardboard box in which there were two young cockerels, one a Poland and the other a Hamburg.

The Poland cockerel is a shaggy-headed, black fellow who trots up and down inside the pen offering battle to the Araucana, who keeps pace with him on the other side of the netting. One day they will have it out, I expect. Araucanas have their own distinctive head adornment and I wonder what a cross would look like. Next summer I may find out. The Hamburg is a wing-trailing, little fellow and quite undaunted by the superior physique of the cock of the walk. He pushes his way into the face of the Araucana as though telling him that if he vanquishes the Poland he will still have a Hamburg to contend with. The bigger they are, the harder they fall. There is no way of persuading cocks that they are simply wasting their substance keeping up with one another and indulging in that endless confrontation. I shall have to make some kind of screen so that they cannot see each other.

The little Hamburg, a golden boy, sticks out his ill-feathered, juvenile neck and crows a high-pitched crow, reminding me of a schoolboy whose voice is newly broken. The Poland does not crow but shakes the feathered topknot out of his eyes every so often. He looks like a slightly punch-drunk boxer. I won't say that birds are like humans in everything they do, but the behaviour of these cockerels sets me laughing out loud. Some people are very like birds.

December 1977

MY recently acquired Poland cockerel is an amusing little fellow whose shaggy "topknot" prevents him from seeing things as well as other birds, and causes him to collide with objects he might otherwise avoid. It is the fringe that makes him nervous, I think, and somewhat highly-strung. He has become very tame and dogs my steps when he fancies I can be persuaded to scatter a little food for him, out of sight of those elephantine old battery hens who come lumbering up to knock him about if he dares to stay to pick a pellet or two. He cocks his head and peers up at me through the hair-like feathering that curtains his eye, and I talk to him, trying to calm his nerves. He crows now and again, but the Araucana cockerel resents his calling and rushes to drive him away. There is nothing I can do to bring about a one-man-one-vote kind of evening up. The cock of the walk is the only one who is entitled to crow, although the very small Hamburg's crowing is ignored, probably because the sound is absurd. The diminutive cockerel's voice hasn't broken properly. His call is high-pitched and effeminate. This dwarf and the Poland keep company. They were raised together and so far in their lives have felt no rivalry.

In the spring I plan to pen them independently so that they can enjoy a full life, each with a mate and a chance to father a brood of chicks. The cock of the walk doesn't know it, but he is becoming redundant. Soon his loud crowing will be heard no more. He has had his day. The Poland will almost certainly inherit the throne.

THE TROUBLESOME MENAGERIE

THE grouping of domestic fowl never ceases to interest me. Now that I have four white silkies, as well as the Araucana group with two cockerels, and the last of my old battery hens, I can watch the alignments. There are two white silkie cockerels and two Araucana cockerels, one of which is the cock of the walk, an older bird with spurs like Turkish sabres. The older cockerel has a harem of ten wives. His son, or grandson – I can't remember where he comes in the generation – has four wives. The old brown hens treat the young cockerel with scant respect and see him off if he comes too close. They tag along with the cock of the walk, chaperoning the younger birds.

The white silkies keep to themselves in the shelter of certain bushes while the cock of the walk strolls in Henry VIII style with his ladies in attendance. The younger cock lurks with his minor harem, hopeful, I suppose, of recruiting one of the less faithful wives of the older bird but never managing to get away with it. At morning feed this No. 2 cockerel has to keep away from the feeding flock. The silkies, pullets and cockerels sometimes have to keep their wits about them too because not only will the old cock give them a drubbing, but the old brown hens may also decide to attack them. One day one of those silkie cockerels will be much bigger than the cock of the walk. When this time comes we may see the order change and the cock of the walk himself skulking in the bushes, his comb dripping blood. This can happen in a free-range world.

January 1980

WHILE the gale rages outside I am sitting at my desk toying with the idea of breeding Sonnerat fowl, if I can get myself a cock and a hen before the breeding season and in time to establish them comfortably in new surroundings. The Sonnerat is the true jungle cock – *Gallus sonneratii* – once frequently encountered (and shot for the pot) by the English Raj when they explored the secret woodlands of the western Ghats. Alas, like the osprey and the sea eagle, the jungle cock became rare due partly to commercial interests.

The feathers of the jungle cock are not only beautiful but much sought after by anglers. For anyone who hasn't seen the jungle cock hackle, Lewis Wright's description of it in his *Illustrated Book of Poultry*, published in the 1880s, cannot be bettered. "The shafts," he said, "expand at the tips into a flat and horny plate which gleams in the sun. These plates are generally of a golden orange colour but occasionally appear banded with various colours. The plumed portion of the hackle is dark greyish, the shafts being deep gold which expand at the tips into plates just described, and not infrequently the hackles will show two such plates, the shaft of the feather contracting after the first and then expanding again." It is against the law to import the feathers of the jungle cock because it is listed as an endangered species, but there is nothing to stop anyone breeding jungle cocks in his backyard. The bird, which resembles the domestic fowl more than Indian game, is, I am assured, quite hardy. The hen, which is without either comb or wattles, will lay two or three separate clutches of four eggs, which, if she will not incubate, may be hatched under a bantam hen.

A gentleman who bred some jungle cocks in 1863 concluded that they needed to be bred early to be forward in condition to withstand our winter. They were otherwise too delicate for this country. On the other hand, I understand that Sonnerat fowl have done well in southern Scotland. In our sheltered situation here they might do even better. Like the bantam, the jungle cock is said to be a tree rooster and quite a flyer. It also has the reputation of being wild; wilder than pen-reared game. One doesn't need to kill it to get the much prized hackles but can follow it about picking them up from the ground when the bird is moulting.

THE TROUBLESOME MENAGERIE

THE existence of colonies of wild honeybees is something about which the average beekeeper is generally unaware. He notices feral pigeons and the domestic cat gone wild, but the renegade bees take themselves off into the wood or the thicket and find themselves a secure home in a hole in some sturdy old tree. In my experience these wild colonies are less aggressive than beehive bees. Few beekeepers ever discover and take the wild colony, but I once helped my grandfather take one. I found it in the trunk of an enormous dead pine tree in the high wood above the farm. I was recruited to help bring the bees and their honey home. We had to cut into the dead wood and the vibration brought the wild bees storming out. We stood knee deep in crumbling wood, found the queen, filled a white enamelled pail with comb, brought most of the bees away with us, and housed them in one of the hives near the farmhouse. The following day they sailed off on the breeze, back up the hill to the wood. They settled high in branches we could never hope to reach, hung about there for perhaps a day, and then vanished.

We never discovered their new dwelling. The honey was of exquisite flavour, sycamore I think, but the old man was resigned to losing the wild colony. It was in their blood, he said, to be wild. Perhaps it was their very wildness that made their honey so good. For my part I was sure their stings were more painful. Although I have found wild colonies here at different times I have never been tempted to storm them and make them domestic.

I CAN'T say that I am built for ballet dancing or that I am good at imitating Charlie Chaplin's walk, but during the week I gave a passable performance. I was busy cutting the grass in the old orchard at the end of which my beehives stand. The rain has encouraged a rank growth round the hives. It seemed to me that afternoon the bees were lying low and I might cut round them – in, out and away in a minute or so. I headed for the end of the path, forgetting that on summer days when bees are not on the flight lines they are generally brooding inside the hive, fed to the gills with the unsuitable weather and ready to vent their spleen on anyone who approaches.

I was in, and almost out and away, before they sent out their anti-terrorist squad who came at me from ground level, stinging me on the backs of both ankles, then on the shins and finally the higher regions of my legs. To crown it all I had a visitor at the time. I did my Swan Lake bit and my Charlie Chaplin impression without my visitor realising I was being anything more than my usual eccentric self.

I recovered my dignity and strolled on behind the grass-cutter as though the phase was one I passed through most days. I have had what might be called my baptism of fire, my most severe stinging of any year since the big snow. If the wiseacres are right about bees I shouldn't suffer from the screws for quite a long time. I can't even pretend, anymore, that I don't feel bee stings.

THE TROUBLESOME MENAGERIE

ABOUT a dozen of my bantams are dedicated tree-roosting birds, and each day towards evening they take themselves off to their perching place above the old henhouse. There seems to be a pecking order in going up into the tree. Certain birds hang about to let others go up first. Perhaps a dominant bird gets the best perch, but the cockerel stays back. He doesn't wait for the last straggler, but flaps into the tree and ascends to his particular branch in stages, while his hens peer down as though waiting to see who the latecomers might be.

I never see their descent in the morning because they do this at first light. Occasionally they are still sheltering under the tree when I go up to open the henhouse, but more often than not the tree-roosting flock stands at the hut awaiting my arrival. I am greeted with much clucking and crooning and flapping about, though the birds from the tree don't follow me into the hut while I ladle out their ration. Each evening when I go to lock up I look into the lower branches of trees near their roost in case one of the flock has decided to perch too close to the ground. This hardly ever happens; if it does, I poke the foolish bird off its perch. It sets up a great cackle, and hens 20 feet up in the holly tree join in.

Last night when I shut up the henhouse a single bird cackled. After peering into the branches for quite a while, I saw her, out on the limb of a wych elm, perhaps ten feet higher up than her companions, roosting among the holly leaves. As I left, this bird flapped down to find a place in the holly, and there was a great lot of indignant cackling that went on and on until I was back at the cottage. When I went upstairs, the last waves of hysteria were diminishing, but I could still hear sporadic cackling from the holly tree. If I hadn't known what it was about, I might have gone hurrying up to see if something was getting at the flock, but these tree roosters are probably safer where they are than others locked up for the night. If a fox or even some smaller predator like an escaped ferret gets into a henhouse, it has the birds at its mercy and kills far more than it can eat.

THE TROUBLESOME MENAGERIE

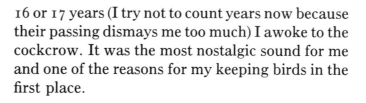

THE crowing of cocks has been known to bring legal battles and provoke everlasting hostility between neighbours, and I am well aware that it is something town-dwellers won't tolerate. Here, distanced from my neighbours by several hundred yards on either side, on an overcast morning in November, the month in which I came into this world, I sit depressed by the silence. There is no cockcrow. My birds haven't flown. I have given them away, betrayed them 'ere the cock crowed thrice, I might say without blasphemy. I was fonder of them than I thought. For

16 or 17 years (I try not to count years now because their passing dismays me too much) I awoke to the cockcrow. It was the most nostalgic sound for me and one of the reasons for my keeping birds in the first place.

How it carried me back to a day when I heard that sound across the rolling farmland of my childhood, a cock of the walk in one place crowing, standing on his midden with head up, listening for the sound to come back to him from another farmyard bird. That world was one of bright sunshine and soft breezes. And then, cocks crowed by moonlight, encouraged by the illumination of the fowlhouse by the moon's rays shafted through cracks in the woodwork, and I would lie awake, taking comfort from the sound. I couldn't tell people just what the cockcrow meant, for they would have laughed at me. I never seemed to have fewer than four crowing cocks, and once the number edged up to 14.

The last cock crowed this week after he came down from the holly tree roost above the old henhouse. He headed a flock of tree-roosting birds that established themselves in the holly tree. I lured him into the pen, and the friend who had agreed to take my birds came and got him, along with eight others. Then, there were seven. The seven were in turn lured into the pen on the following morning. The daily chore of letting birds out and feeding them has ended. I shall miss my birds, for I was very fond of them as individuals and I shall certainly miss the cockcrow for a long time.

A CAT CALLED TOPSY

Both cats and dogs were part of my life as a child, but I grew up to have a greater affection for dogs. The cat's independence did not appeal to me then. When I married we had two dogs before Susy came on the scene. Susy was wished upon us by my father who adored his own little Cairn terrier. She came uninvited, all the way by train from Inverness. Soon, she took charge of the family and became the dog of my life. We moved to my father's cottage when he died and the pine wood and the limestone cliff became Susy's hunting ground. She lived to be 15½ and I miss her still, though she died over 12 years ago.

I became a cat man when my wife tamed a semi-wild cat that had killed several of my young pheasants that poked their heads through the wire netting of the pen. The cat killer came indoors and had a litter of kittens in a cupboard in the kitchen. The smallest and most highly-strung of the litter — whom we named Topsy — remained with us when the others were given away. I fell in love with her and she became the cat of my life. When we moved we had advice from people all over the world, among them Johnny Morris, a man with great feeling for animals and concern for their welfare. Topsy is nearly 12 years old now, and still hunts as happily in the wilderness here as she did in Wales.

A CAT CALLED TOPSY

THE last of the wild cat's litter turns out to be a cat with a character all its own. It has the bone structure of the Siamese and something of the Siamese's liking for vertical ascents of trees, curtains or anything climbable. It loves water. Obviously one of the mysteries of its cat existence is the true nature of those brilliant drips coming from a tap not properly turned off. Water can be patted and it splatters about like molten lead or solder. It makes rings and eddies into which a curious cat can peer and see a diffused image of itself, projected there as though by some

genius of the cinema striving for special effects. When the water becomes still the magic is gone. The little black cat, made of delicate springs and as lean as a wild ass, goes scampering away, hardly touching the ground but bouncing, ricocheting, cannoning at high speed and coming back on its own track almost before its shadow has passed. I wonder about it, for it loves feathers, bags of feathers stolen from my fly-tying cabinet. Mallard wing, pheasant tail or a bowed hackle light as thistledown, are all a delight to the playful little creature. I scold it and it looks up at me without comprehending what I am trying to say.

This is what a four- or five-ounce kitten's life is about. There is no other world. I think about it and find myself being persuaded that there is a philosophy here, a kitten philosophy which one might apply to human existence. There should be complete abandonment now and again. Man should lose himself in a game and forget the rate bill, inflation and the cost of living. Time is really a device contrived by a tedious mind. Labour is the opposite of pleasure. A kitten plays with a ball of crushed paper and sleeps like a dead thing afterwards. The world is a warm, comfortable place or a self-made nightmare. In a way I am relieved that the last of the litter is bespoke, as the tailors used to call it. An elderly couple have sent a message from Shropshire asking us to keep the little one for a month until they can come and take it away. That little black bomb will change someone else's life if it doesn't change ours. It is in its nature to take charge of people.

A CAT CALLED TOPSY

THE black kitten, growing a bit and looking more panther-lean than ever, is in everything. She waters the greenhouse with me. She paints a beehive. We get on so long as I do things her way, but I am disconcerted to think that she is a reincarnated gardener, house painter, carpenter and beer brewer. The other day she popped into my son's car, sounded the horn by banging it with her forepaw and then, not sure whether the note was right or not, paused and considered before sounding the horn again. Having done this, she jumped into the boot of the car, looked round and jumped out again. She could have been a mechanic in some previous existence.

On the other hand I think she had something to do with glazing or roofing. When I set about the task of renovating the disused greenhouse with polythene, I was surprised to find the kitten taking more than usual interest. She scaled the glazing timbers and delicately moved from one place to another, while I struggled and swore when the wind flapped the polythene and made it sail in the air like an enormous bridal train. The kitten knew how, but it was a matter of communication and I am not very good at that where cats are involved. The kitten went off for her siesta and came back to inspect the work at the end of that very hot day. She seemed to approve. We went back indoors together, where she wanted me to operate the washing machine for some reason. One of her little tricks is hooking out the draining arm. I feel that one day she will switch the thing on and take a ride in the spin drier.

WHEREVER I go I find I am stalked by the cat. She is of course no ordinary moggy, but a black panther, a loping huntress that should really be accompanied by at least one bewhiskered attendant in a turban. She crouches down and waits to ambush me with her tail gently swaying, but changes her mind at the last minute and, instead of pouncing upon me, dashes away across the rough grass and then straight up the trunk of the nearest pine until she is 10 or 12 feet up. I ignore the danger of being taken unawares and mauled to death, even when she does her stalking at dusk, and I come down the path after locking up the hens, lighting my way with the lantern. I see her eyes in the black background and I am thankful that she isn't much more than 20 inches long from the tip of her nose to the tip of her tail.

Only rarely will she let me swoop on her and pick her up, but when I catch her she consents to be carried like an infant, her forepaws crossed and her large eyes studying the trees as we pass under them. I am not sure that I haven't been bewitched and that this lithe, incredibly fleet cat isn't someone's familiar. Her stare is disconcerting to the point of making me self-conscious, but then she becomes a panther or a tigress again and sharpens her claws on a tree and walks with the dignity of the Bengali. With all her seeming wildness and high spirits she never inflicts the slightest scratch. If Susy was the dog of my life this lean cat has set herself to be the cat of my life. Once again I am trapped by an animal.

A CAT CALLED TOPSY

WE just had to name the cat, for it was confusing her to be called first one thing and then another. I have always had a weakness for nicknames for everyone in the family, but these are never consistently applied. Although the inconsistency didn't bother the family, the cat was another matter and she has now become Topsy. She will no longer be called Skip, Skipper or Cadler. When we had our Cairn she got well used to being summoned as Susy, Sue, Wog and Wogger, but people looked oddly at me at times. I was aware that they considered me a little eccentric and did not appreciate that the odd names were an indication of my affection for the little dog. My weakness for nicknames was brought home to me on an occasion when I came off the mountain with my son and we struck up an acquaintance with a man who had been climbing. When we went to quench our thirst after the day's exertions, our new-found friend turned to me and asked: "And what will Fred have?" I looked blankly at him, and he stared at me in return. "Fred? Oh Fred. Yes, Fred will have a glass of cider," I stuttered, and "Fred" laughed so much that I am sure we were both privately labelled mad. So Topsy is Topsy and will never grow up with any other name.

The question of a name came up the day before yesterday when we took the cat to the vet's surgery so that she could be neutered. The young lady who carried her off in the wire cage needed a name, it seemed. Perhaps cats, like newborn babies, sometimes get mixed up in surgery? Poor Topsy was shaken by her ordeal, and I wondered if she would ever play with a feather again, or stalk me on my morning trip to let out the hens. Young animals have great powers of recovery however, and I need not have worried. Although she slept yesterday away and did not eat or drink, at night she had a meal of liver and her milk. This morning she was waiting to go up to the hens as usual. We even had one of her ambushes, which are sometimes the whole purpose of the journey.

Nearly all domestic pets are creatures of habit to an extent only their owners can really appreciate. Topsy has grafted herself on to the domestic set-up in the same way that Susy did in her day, and I am beginning to learn that while cats are cats, they are not entirely motivated by cupboard love.

A CAT CALLED TOPSY

THE trouble with Topsy, our scaled-down black panther of a cat, is that she once managed to catch and kill a full-grown wood pigeon. I suspect that she worked her way up a tree on the branch of which the unfortunate woodie was roosting, and seized the bird before it knew what had happened. Ever since, Topsy has had an ambition to catch something big. A blackbird would do, but she really fancies the cock pheasant. This big, fluffed-out fellow looks like a miniature turkey cock when he stalks down the path and through the hens. He locates other cock pheasants by making his *cok-cok* call. Topsy hears this and has come to associate the sound with a new opportunity to try her hunting skill on a worthwhile prey. She walks as gently as a fly on butter. She takes her time.

A cock pheasant has the most acute hearing. If a fox can hear a human heart beat, which I am inclined to think it can, a cock pheasant is sensitive to the smallest vibration, the dying sound wave from ten miles away. The cat, too, orientates herself in relation to her quarry simply by picking up the smallest sound. The cat and the bird become motionless. It is stalemate. The cat may make a dash to cover 15 or 20 feet, but the bird can launch himself almost vertically. If Topsy ever succeeds she will be hooked on the thing for life, even though she may only eliminate a cock pheasant who lacked what it takes to survive in this world. I hope she fails. She will get so much more enjoyment out of trying.

A CAT CALLED TOPSY

IN the jungle on the top of the cliff we have one or two old and somewhat stunted yew trees, none of them much more than ten feet in height, I seemed to remember. I thought one of them might provide me with a large enough piece of wood to carve a full-sized decoy duck, and so I decided to go up and see what I could find. Going into the jungle is exactly that. The blackthorn, the bramble, the dog rose and every other sort of sprawling thorn bars the way. The path I clear from time to time soon closes in. A tendril of blackberry loops across the gap, threads itself into the bushes on the other side, and puts down a second root, layering itself naturally. The cleared path becomes a kind of seedbed in which other thorn-bearing shrubs take root. The cutting in one season stimulates growth before the second arrives, and it isn't a question of making a path so much as keeping a pathway.

I went up with a pair of stout gloves on my hands and a pair of secateurs to help me get through. Topsy came with me, treading gently like a black jungle cat, and pausing every so often to look at me with her large yellow-green eyes. We were in our wild element, although I am neither as keen-sighted nor as sensitive to sound and scent as the cat. Each time I stopped to deal with the trailing thorns, Topsy stopped. She was in no hurry. A small bird flitted over and perched on a thorn up ahead. She tensed and watched it. The bird wasn't afraid of me, but when it spotted my companion it fled. I cut a path all the way to the cliff in front of the old tower, and passed two bushy yews on the way. One of them had been topped long ago and had grown thick and bushy at the base as a result. Its trunk was large enough in diameter for my purpose, but I hesitated to go for the chainsaw. I find it hard to bring myself to cut down a living tree of any sort. I decided to make a wider search for a dead yew. On the way back down Topsy, who had stayed within a few feet of me until then, made sudden dashes and swarmed away up into thin branches of sapling ash and hazel. She fancies herself on the trapeze. Perhaps she is training to bring herself to a pitch where she can catch a squirrel in his natural element, but she lacks the nimbleness of the squirrel, which is just as well. She may have nine lives, but where a squirrel can survive a fall of 50 feet, a cat might not.

A CAT CALLED TOPSY

WHEN I was quite small I used to recite a poem about a little shadow that went everywhere with me. I cannot think who the poet was, or if it was just a bit of nursery doggerel, but it applies today. Topsy is my shadow and has been all day. I cannot make a move without her. She pads at my heel, or goes a pace in front of me like a sleek black panther. This morning she was particularly proud of herself because she had made a kill. We stopped while she showed it to me, patting it with her forepaws as though it might have been a hot scone on a girdle. It was a pretty-as-paint chaffinch, but a cat is a cat and chaffinches fall as often as sparrows. My shadow got under my feet when I was digging the garden. The trouble is that she does not appreciate what I am about. She presses forward to study the spit of earth I am lifting. If a worm wriggles out of it, she must pat that and try to make it join in some kind of game she improvises. I talk to her but she does not choose to listen; cats have a wonderful way of showing their single-mindedness. She hampered my diligent efforts to be the poor man's Percy Thrower until I gave up digging. But alas, she is just as enthusiastic about getting under my feet if I try to do something else.

When she had frustrated my spadework, she galloped to the bean frame and scaled it at top speed to peer down at me while I tried to do a little work with the handfork. She must not be out of things, but I was startled when she came flying through the air, almost hitting me on the head in a wild leap down to the cold frame. This is covered with polythene. She went right through it and surfaced a moment later like a dog hauling itself out of a river. I scolded her, but her policy is to convince me she does not know right from wrong, and has no intention of learning. I can interpret what she does in only one other way – she does not care what I think. We will get on like a house on fire providing my way is her way.

It is quite impossible to prevent cats getting their own way. They are two jumps ahead in everything, and sometimes more. I trained a gundog once and was very proud of my work, but cats are different. Anyone who says he is a cat-trainer must be a bit of a Munchhausen. I am convinced of that. No one trains cats. Cats train people.

A CAT CALLED TOPSY

FROM the window in front of my desk the view is a somewhat restricted one. I smile to think of the small room itself being described as a "study", for it could never be anything as pretentious as that. It was, in fact, a small dressing room adjoining the bedroom, and its single window is four feet from the floor and about 18 inches by 12 inches, hardly a window on the world but enough, I suppose, to keep my thoughts from wandering too far. At the moment I have a view of the wych elms of the hedge, now 30 feet high, and the walnut tree that is one of a line of three planted along the wall that adjoins the hedge. The fluttering leaves are not much of a distraction, but I ponder on the walnut crop when I see them, still green yet, bobbing as the branches are disturbed by the wind. A pair of squirrels track through the walnut branches, occasionally stopping to mark their territory in the manner of foxes and many other wild creatures, and I marvel at their confident progress up and down the thicker branches. They are not consciously indulging in acrobatics or aerobatics when they travel through the thinner stems, or occasionally take leaps into space to save time going down and coming up again. The squirrels resent the magpie that drops on to the top of the walnut tree and perches there, swaying a little precariously, but with no anxiety because at a movement of its short wings it can swim in the air and steady itself once more. The two creatures aren't rivals, but they are wary of one another. I suppose the squirrel knows the voracious habits of the whole crow tribe, while the magpie knows that the grey squirrel is not averse to devouring helpless chicks.

The third occupant of the trees outside my window is Topsy, our cat, and she, it seems, envies the squirrel's ability to make such rapid progress through the branches and up the vertical trunk. At times she is prompted to emulate them. She makes a tiger dash at the tree and runs right up the trunk simply clawing her way aloft until the impetus of her initial dash is spent. After this, if she catches sight of me, she goes a little higher as though inviting me to admire her progress, and I do admire her until I become anxious for her safety. Cats have nine lives and can survive a fall, though not, I think, such falls as I have seen squirrels take in their-stride. I stop looking out of the window and deliberately ignore the climbing cat. I expect she is put down and disappointed, like a showing-off schoolboy when this happens, but I do not want to encourage her and I certainly do not want to see her fall.

A CAT CALLED TOPSY

November 1976

THE cat and the bird go together in my mind like the cat and the mouse. I suppose the average cat catches as many of one sort as the other. Topsy, perhaps because of the nature of our ground, accounts for more rodents of one sort and another than she does feathered prey, but I am sorry to say that the birds she brings home are usually of a species I would preserve. The blackbird is too old a hand to be caught by the cat, and the bullfinch also is too wary to be taken. The jay and the magpie are in the same line of business. Topsy has to be content with what she can get, a robin, poor thing, a chaffinch and, the other day, a goldcrest. The goldcrest is not uncommon here. It seems to like the sort of trees and brush we have around. It is probably as well-equipped to survive as the wren that emulates the mouse, and explores every hole and crevice in the limestone wall.

Topsy arrived on the scene with the small bird in her mouth. I must say she has a soft mouth. She would have been highly-prized for the gentle way she carries had she been a cocker or a springer spaniel, but a cat she is, and cats are not concerned with delivering a bird to their master's knee. Topsy contrives to put her prey on the ground and gently coax it to move and show signs of life. She does this with a sideways pat with her paw that is strangely touching to watch. There is nothing vicious about it from the time it begins until her "victim" dies of shock, which we, of course, attempt to prevent when we can get close enough to her to intervene. The goldcrest fluttered and got away and we rescued it. Topsy did not complain.

She was curious about what we seemed to be going to do with it, but did not attempt to get it back. On most occasions no matter what the owner of the cat may do, the bird dies of shock. My wife, however, managed to keep the goldcrest warm until it perked up. It suddenly flew off, but had to be caught again because there was no way of directing it to an open window. In the end it was placed in a bush growing by the side of the lane. Shortly afterwards it flew off to more satisfactory cover, which pleased us enormously.

Topsy had forgotten she had ever caught it in the first place. Cats are like that. They live for the moment and do not brood about things. Yesterday I was horrified to see her 50 feet above ground on the trunk of a pine tree. She had gone up after a grey squirrel which had, in the meantime, emigrated to another part of the wood and scolded her from a distance. She came down slowly, backwards, moving like a sloth. Five minutes later she was indoors eating her breakfast as though nothing had happened. Like the goldcrest, the squirrel had gone from her mind and even the danger she had been in was a thing of the past.

A CAT CALLED TOPSY

WHERE I go, Topsy goes. She does her best to stand in for the dog I should have, and shows an interest, or a cat's curiosity, in whatever I am doing. During the week I found a cowl on the kitchen gable had been bitten through by the fierceness of anthracite fumes from the stove. It needed to be taken down, and I got the ladder out and climbed up to see what I could do. I was busy trying to dislodge the cowl when something brushed my arm and Topsy was there, poking her nose in to see what my problem was. I scolded her but she chose to look blankly at me, as though wondering if I was afraid of falling from the ladder. I got down, brought the cowl with me, and went back up again to tidy up the chimney pot which had got some wire round it and a broken fillet of cement which needed to be removed. Topsy was there in a flash, her tail brushing my face as she had a look down the chimney.

After this I wasn't surprised to find her assisting me when I was up the ladder repairing the long greenhouse. She is a jack of all trades. She will supervise my clearing the grate. She likes to see how a fly is tied. She has walked across the typewriter, to see what I have written I suppose, and she to's and fro's to accompany me when I chop sticks, plant a few onion sets (which I have to cover with netting to stop her recultivating the patch) or go to feed the hens. How can I explain to her that I like to be by myself sometimes? She has a way of ignoring complaints and hearing only the things she wants to hear.

A CAT CALLED TOPSY

May 1977

A SEDENTARY cat is a sad creature, I feel, and misses a great deal. It is debatable whether any animal should be kept simply in creature comfort, although there are many wretched animals roaming free. Topsy, I am pleased to say, has the best of both worlds. She comes in to stretch languorously before a big fire, to slip off and curl up in the "pitcher" linen basket (which has become a cat basket) or help herself to supper freshly laid out for her. She has a number of ambitions. I think I have them in proper order of priority when I list them as catching the seagull which comes to feed at our window, catching a squirrel that runs 60 feet to the top of a pine, and swears at her as she swarms up the rough bark after it, catching a cock pheasant that knows all about cats slinking on their bellies to take it unawares, catching a particular white muscovy duck or, well down the scale, a bantam hen that reacts hysterically and thereby encourages further attempts.

Topsy patrols like a panther and is always hopeful, but we would have her no other way. She must come and go when the mood takes her. Even when the kitchen window is open, and she can come in that way, she will pad round to the French window and patter her forepaws on the glass – to be admitted, not through the window, but by the door. We let her in with great patience, but I begin to think that she is now walking over us, trying to discover what further liberties she may take with us – but what a dull life it would be for all of us if she snoozed her days away.

TALKING about gulls, a friend in New England writes: "We were interested in your account of your prowling Topsy and her desire to destroy the gull. Not long ago a cat cornered Gussie, our resident gull, against our bulkhead, holding her with one paw and slashing at her with the other just like a pugilist. Meanwhile Gussie was flapping her wings in an attempt to get away, but making no attempt to assault the cat with her formidable beak. I think the cat would have killed her had I not intervened."

This kind of confrontation happened occasionally with our ducks. Topsy never went in with the intention of killing, and no casualty ever resulted. The duck always managed to escape unhurt. In the case of the drake, Topsy was always forced to give ground. Despite her frantic rushes at the gull I doubt whether she would follow through and kill the bird, unless she got into some kind of frenzy in the process. I begin to wish she would show more interest in the gulls now that we have twice as many as before.

A CAT CALLED TOPSY

WHAT is there about running water and dripping taps that so fascinates a cat? Topsy can be relied upon to sit for minutes on end staring at a dripping tap. Perhaps it is the disappearance of the droplet that intrigues, but water holds some special magic for her, and always has done. Countless times in summer she will get herself drenched when I use a hose or a watering can in the greenhouse. I have often laughed about it and wondered if she hasn't a bit of otter in her, although cats hate getting wet and Topsy doesn't stay in the line of fire for very long.

A reader who lives in Denmark tells me that her cats are similarly hypnotised by water. Perhaps it is part of the cat's inheritance? Some dogs love to play in water and enjoy getting drenched, but cats are mystified over the apparent transformation of solid into liquid, the growth of a water drip on a tap, its fall and then its complete disappearance. Nothing, they seem to say, can vanish into thin air like this. I have seen puzzled dogs but most dogs shrug mysteries off without much pondering.

Topsy will go to the back of the television set when something she saw going out of sight seemed likely to have escaped through the back of the box. She has the same thoughtful expression when she fails to find anything behind the set. The secrets of nature and science may be too much for a dog, but a cat wants to unravel them, or appears to give them serious consideration.

A CAT CALLED TOPSY

THERE are times on a cool evening when I have built a too large fire and conditions tend to induce a kind of haze or half-sleep from which the heraldic noise of the news bulletin on television barely awakens me and only some major disturbance can bring me to my senses. The other evening the fire and the double insurance against the cold – a drop of whisky – had just about achieved their purpose when we heard a knocking sound. In such a quiet house there is nothing that makes this kind of noise but some living creature, and on investigation it was discovered that the culprit was Topsy. Topsy had had singular success in her hunting that evening and had popped through the window first with a small vole and then with a shrew, both of which,

bewildered by success, she had foolishly let go free. The vole had shown an amazing turn of speed and vanished from the hall, heading for the dining room. The shrew, in turn, had slipped off along the side of the fitted carpet. My wife came to report this second happening but I assured her the shrew would now die of fright. Shrews are well known to be highly strung and will die at the drop of a hat. I become wonderfully inventive when I don't want to be disturbed. Topsy had no doubt found the vole and popped out with it, but, of course, she hadn't. She had gone out to find a fresh one. Not finding it, there she was, hunting the one that had escaped into the dining room, and where was the vole? It was in the grandfather clock!

My son hurried to see what all the clatter was about and opened the door of the clock. Topsy plunged in headfirst and the pendulum rattled on the case. She squirmed and turned and came out again without her prize. Just as my son located the vole, Topsy dived in again. A moment later she reversed ends and put her forepaws on the door frame. The vole was across her mouth like a moustache. She sprang neatly out of the clock and dashed into the hall. The front door was opened and she went off out to supper. We still have a shrew somewhere under the carpet. Without any kind of shrew detector we shall have to wait until it shows itself. Topsy isn't really interested in shrews, and only brings them in to show us she has her wits about her.

A CAT CALLED TOPSY

September 1978

TREATING an animal with the same consideration one may display towards a human is, for some people, an eccentricity and even a source of irritation. I have been guilty of this intolerance myself on many occasions, for seeing myself as others see me is not one of my particular talents. I know well enough that the dogs I have owned from time to time crept into my affection and became more respected as I got to know them, or, as some people would have it, became more doting upon them. Susy, our Cairn terrier, spent a lifetime achieving her ambition to sleep on the bed. Topsy, our green-eyed, sooty Burmese cat, quickly laid claim to a place at the bottom of the bed, and, moving over again and again to lie against my feet, has sometimes forced me to get out of my bed before the next movement made me fall out of it. I can imagine the snorts of scorn some people might greet me with were I to go further and confess how much I go out of my way to accommodate a cat upon which I really dote.

I am not alone, however. I am sure there are many hundreds of people in the same boat, possibly thousands who see nothing wrong in treating their dog, cat, bird, or even their donkey with self-indulgent and seemingly misguided affection. The motives are something a psychologist would list with analytical precision and objectivity – unless he happened to be hooked on the same thing. I may not have let my dog eat from my plate but I have shared my meal with it. Many shepherds and shooting men share their snack with the dog and the business of doing so goes all the way back to the cave. I don't share the bathroom with my pet. The cat sometimes pops her head in and wonders what I am doing splashing water over myself. Susy occasionally used to scratch on the bathroom door but what she wanted was what other members of the family wanted – myself out of there.

A relative visiting us the other day told me an amusing story of his recently acquired spaniel, an animal upon which both he and his wife dote abjectly. After receiving dental treatment and being sent home with a set of new teeth, which the dentist said might give a little trouble at first, the owner of the spaniel found that what the dentist had said was true. His new plate pained him and had to be removed. The denture was placed on the side of the washbasin and left there. In the meantime its owner went off to breakfast as well as he could without it. Shortly afterwards his inquisitive spaniel, a born retriever of almost anything not too heavy to carry, bustled into the breakfast room with the discarded denture in its mouth. Alas, the set of teeth had seemed more like a chewy object than a chewing device. The denture was so chewed up that the gleaming white teeth fell out of the mangled plate and the dentist had to go to work all over again, but what could anyone say but "There's a clever dog!"?

A CAT CALLED TOPSY

THERE are people who take their cats for a walk as other people exercise their dogs on collar and lead, and I sometimes wonder if I shouldn't have "broken" Topsy to collar and lead so that we could explore the countryside and walk the footpath together, for she is a great walker at heel and will plod after me wherever I go. This may just be ordinary cat behaviour I had failed to notice before Topsy came on the scene.

Yesterday, thinking there might be a few late-ripening blackberries on the field adjoining the footpath, or perhaps a horse mushroom or two, I plodded off up to the stile to see what I could find. Topsy must have spotted my departure, for when I turned my head to look back as I neared the stile, there she was at heel, her tail straight up in the air. She was delighted to be with me. She sprang on to the top of the stone stile before I could get to the first step and then sprang down to lead me on. We crossed the adjoining meshwire fence and went down through the bushes into the open field together. I looked for blackberries and found none. Topsy kept an eye on the bullocks as they converged upon us, but kept her tail up. We went on and on, and I began to wonder just how far she would have gone had I not turned back when we neared the home territory of my neighbour's three collies and his springer spaniel.

Topsy is obviously a cat that likes to walk and have company. This kind of excursion could be made every day, I am sure. When she hunts she is an entirely different animal and travels alone, half-running through the orchard, barely turning her head to give me a greeting, and doing her own thing with extraordinary single-mindedness. One day we must go on a long walk together, and I may be able to discover if she has territorial limits beyond which she will not go.

A CAT CALLED TOPSY

CATS and owls are equally at home in the dark and must, in the course of their nocturnal travels, be aware of one another. One keeping to the trees and the other hunting on the ground they are hardly likely to be in confrontation very often, which is a good thing for both since the owl's beak and talons are as useful weapons as the cat's claws and fangs. I was out in the court the other evening after darkness and stayed out when I heard the tawny owls calling out to one another in the pine trees.

There was a lot to talk about on this particular evening and I encouraged the conversation by cupping my hands and making a suitable sound which the tawnies seemed to think worth answering, but what intrigued me was Topsy's reaction. She stared up into the pines, switched her tail and set herself as though she might spring 30 or 40 feet into the air to put the owls out of there. As often happens when I make my owl noises, one or two of the birds moved closer, flitting quickly to branches from which they could locate the sound better. I could see the black outline of one particular owl as he perched on a bare limb. He turned his head and bowed a little as though listening for all he was worth. Perhaps he heard my heart beating, for I believe that not only owls but foxes have this acute kind of hearing, but Topsy wasn't at any disadvantage so far as her "locating" equipment was concerned. All at once she sprang from the court on to the wall above which the pines grow and made a dash for the nearest tree. It was not by accident that it was one in which an owl was perched. She clawed her way aloft with her characteristic agility and speed and was perhaps 25 feet up before the owl launched itself and made a quick flit to the next tree. Topsy hung on there rather despairingly, I thought, and then slowly descended like a boy coming down from a rook's nest. The owls went on talking.

A CAT CALLED TOPSY

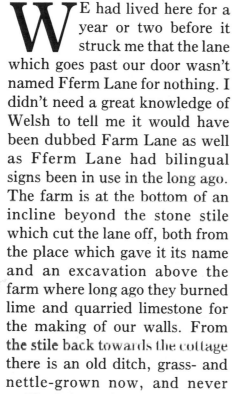

WE had lived here for a year or two before it struck me that the lane which goes past our door wasn't named Fferm Lane for nothing. I didn't need a great knowledge of Welsh to tell me it would have been dubbed Farm Lane as well as Fferm Lane had bilingual signs been in use in the long ago. The farm is at the bottom of an incline beyond the stone stile which cut the lane off, both from the place which gave it its name and an excavation above the farm where long ago they burned lime and quarried limestone for the making of our walls. From the stile back towards the cottage there is an old ditch, grass- and nettle-grown now, and never holding any water. Blackthorns hedge the ditch in and only wild creatures, or a sheep that occasionally bursts through from the field down below, know what it is like in the secret tunnel of the thorns. Once or twice over the years I have seen a bird running on the footpath and taking cover in the blackthorns and identified it as a water rail.

Yesterday while I was warming myself beside the Aga, Topsy suddenly popped through the little window above the sink, looking for a minute as though she had grown a large and rather bushy dark brown moustache. I thought she had come in with a blackbird, but the bird proved to be nothing so commonplace. It was a water rail, and I was glad to think I had been in the kitchen when Topsy arrived for I was able to rescue it from her unharmed. The rail had been caught in the ditch, I think. It was very cold, and not in any condition to run as it normally would have done, and I put it into a large brown paper bag which I hung from the side of the cupboard near the Aga, keeping the bag in place by setting the teapot on its upper end. This made a kind of hammock for the rail and I left it hanging there until the warmth of the room restored it to its personal comfort. Topsy was off out by this time, looking for something else, and I was able to take the rail to the ditch and release it. It flew the way this species always does, rather heavily with legs dangling, until it made a landing in the undergrowth of the ditch. I was pleased with myself.

Rails don't come my way every day; indeed, not many people see them, though they may hear them and mistake them for corncrake when they call in the dusk. When they nest they lay about the same number of eggs as the moorhen, but a much smaller egg, creamy white in colour with an odd small brownish spot or two on it, although I must say I have only once found the nest (by accident) and have nothing with which to make comparison. The eggs, as I recall them, were about the same size as those of the corncrakes I found as a boy in Galloway.

A CAT CALLED TOPSY

October 1981

FRIENDS tell me that I am so besotted by Topsy that I should write a book about her, as I did for Susy, our much loved Cairn, but Susy was a much less complicated character. It isn't impossible to read a dog's mind. A cat is an altogether different kettle of fish and not only has contrariness but an inscrutable expression. My portrait of Topsy would undoubtedly end up as a gallery of cats, all black with the most lovely grape-green eyes, and all different. I look at tigers and see them with something of Topsy about them. There is one that runs along a beach or sometimes through snow, doing its bit for the ad-men who work for the oil moguls. Now that tiger could be Topsy, lithe and lean, as smoothly running as a blood horse, animal perfection in motion. There are other times when she sits up looking to the front with the dignity and phlegm of a lion, her eyes almost hooded. A blue tit or a wren drops down into the court and she is transformed. Her tail gives a twitch. Her eyes reflect the light in a baleful way. She is a fierce huntress and has forsaken the bowl of cream and the cat-food dish.

We are simply used by the cat, for when she has no time for us she stalks away. When she comes indoors, in the absence of a mouse or a bird she has stalked in the bush, she winds herself round my legs, purring. Ah, she loves me, I say, but I am deluding myself. She wants the dish or she is simply drying her damp fur on my trousers. And yet she talks to us and we begin to understand the language. She wants the rain turned off, a door opened. Perversely she insists upon a particular door being opened even when she may come in by a window and scratches on the French windows to get this done. I doubt whether she would come through the French windows, the catches on which are rather stiff and difficult to operate. She has to be let into the hall by what we call the front door although it adjoins what we call the back door.

A book about Topsy would have to mention her invisibility in the shadow of bushes or in the potting shed if I happen to lock it up, for she has a way of making herself unseen that baffles me and sometimes baffles the creatures she hunts. I have to go out to the shed when Topsy is missing and unlock the door to discover if she has been imprisoned there. She streaks past me. I don't even see the going of her. By the time I return to the fireside, she has stolen my seat.

A CAT CALLED TOPSY

NOTHING delights Topsy more than to have persuaded either my wife or myself to accompany her on a promenade through the garden, up to the hens or into the long greenhouse.

She evinces her pleasure on these occasions in a variety of ways. Sometimes she will pause, catch a pine cone in her forepaws and toss it in the air. Sometimes she will skip in a most erratic fashion, spring up on all four feet and land a pace to the right or left, or she will crouch down like a tigress waiting to spring, half-hiding in the shelter of a large stone but never remaining there for more than a minute before racing away. It is the sheer joy of living that makes her perform these antics. When she doesn't do them, she will rush to one of the standard lilac trees and stretch upwards to

sharpen her claws on its well-shredded bark, for she hardly misses a day to give it a claw-raking. Her *pièce de résistance* is often reserved for a welcoming home. She will come dashing past, head uphill to one of the pines and, at a gallop in which she must extend and retract her claws at an incredible speed, rush high up the tree. This climb never looks like one because it is so rapid that she appears to ascend like a fly running up a wall.

Almost all of these things can take place on a walk, but to prove that she is really an outdoor cat she will join me when I have been up in the wood for some time on my own, and attempt to lead me on to some other, more remote corner of the jungle. Here, she seems to be trying to tell me, we both belong. We have no need for the kitchen and the Aga's radiated heat, or even the smell of onions being fried, which she loves because she associates it with her favourite treat – liver. No, we belong in the wild, and if I stay out there she will remain to keep me company.

When I head away from the house she heads in the same direction. She often abandons me, even on a wet day, if I show that I am going home. I have only had one cat in my life, and so perhaps what I am saying about Topsy is what other people's cats do all the time, but I can't believe that every cat is like every other one. Topsy was born of a wild mother who was coaxed indoors and had her litter in the kitchen, next to the Aga. Topsy has always exhibited a certain wildness and love of the open. She wouldn't be my cat if she didn't.

A CAT CALLED TOPSY

WHILE I was waiting for my wife at the supermarket the other morning I got in the way of a woman who was pushing a trolley loaded with tins of catfood. She said she was getting them in in case we got snowed up. Her cat was one of those snooze-by-the-fire animals, it seemed, and wouldn't bestir itself to go out and catch something in an emergency. Snow suits Topsy. It is conducive to the softly, softly approach, when birds aren't hard to catch.

The woman trundled her great load of tins to her car, leaving me wondering what we did before the supermarket began loading shelves with cat brand-names too numerous to mention. I can remember long ago being asked to get rabbits for our farm cats who were very skilled hunters and could catch things for themselves, when they weren't being mollycoddled. Dogs had their meat from the knackers' yard in those days, and marrowbones and scraps from the butcher.

In London I remember cat's meat men and cat's meat shops. I had a landlady who bothered me a little because she was always "just off down the road for a penn'orth o' cats' meat". She didn't have a cat, and I told her I was a faddist. I didn't like things like hot pot, lob scouse, Irish stew, curry or shepherd's pie. The lady didn't put my mind at rest, and I had to discover for myself she doted on cats but had some kind of allergy.

When I see Topsy coming across the court, the way she did this morning, with a mouse across her mouth like a drooping moustache, I wish she wouldn't do it. If I had shares in one of the catfood concerns, I would probably lobby my Member of Parliament and get him to promote a bill to have all cats belled. Without that vested interest (why is vested interest somehow shameful?), I am against bells on cats, as I am against collars on hunting dogs. A belled cat must be one of the most frustrated creatures in the world. A hunting dog can be hung up by his collar or get the thing hitched on a tree root underground.

But to return to the subject of cats and their feeding. Of late, Topsy has come to plague me to show her favour by giving her a token from my supper tray. She will force herself to eat something she normally wouldn't take. We have an established ritual, and generally a token is all that is expected, but there are some things she will eat until her eyes pop, such as cold turkey, cold lamb, cold pork and liver. If my supper happens to be a hot dish, I have to respond to her patting my leg (with her claws out) and drop her a piece of meat. She advances to the morsel, pats it with her paw, and then springs back from it to sit staring until she decides it is cool enough to be eaten. I never manage to persuade her a thing isn't hot. She ignores what I say. It may be instinctive caution, or the fact that she feels heat radiating with greater sensitivity than I have, but of course man is the only animal that cooks food and eats it hot.

A CAT CALLED TOPSY

THE final consensus on cat-moving is that cats are more attached to their owners than to their territory and, provided they are moved along with familiar objects and introduced to their new habitat with a degree of common sense, all will be well. A tranquillising pill helps. Among the stack of reassuring letters I received were two or three that contained warnings about disasters that might befall the cat-mover.

One reader mentioned sad advertisements she had noted from time to time in local newspapers where a cat-owner appealed for help in recovering a pet escaped *en route* to its new home. Cats have more than a little of Houdini in them, or perhaps Houdini studied how they made their escape from boxes and baskets? A cat that breaks loose is usually terrified. Once it is away it is almost impossible to recapture.

A friend I talked to about this mentioned how he had once stopped to converse with a friend who was on his way to Ireland with the family cat for company. The cat slipped through a narrow space above a partly wound-up car window and dashed away like a streak of light into adjoining gardens. The traveller missed the ferry; his cat was never seen again.

The other hazard, it would seem, is in taking a cat to a territory dominated by the fox, for even the wariest cat has to learn the danger areas and the ways of Old Charley. One of my correspondents told me how a cat she had moved vanished with-

out trace, leaving a freshly killed bird on the path. While the cat was stalking her prey the fox was still hunting. Topsy, I am quite sure, knows about the fox. Occasionally she has come in at night, big-eyed with her tail as bushy as a bottle brush, and I have guessed she had been a jump or two ahead of the fox. In her new domain, when she gets there, foxes abound. My late father-in-law, protecting his young gamebirds, once shot half a dozen in one evening, and I am sure the local master of the hunt never spoke to him again. I might invite the huntsman to put hounds through our five-acre jungle once in a while for Topsy's sake if he wants to be in my good books.

A CAT CALLED TOPSY

TOPSY, in a skittish mood this morning, dodged past me into the potting shed where such order as I once had has disappeared and given place to packages and bundles, things tied together and packed into tea chests in preparation for our eventual removal.

I swear our boss-cat knows what she is about. She waits until the door is almost closed before she streaks through it, and once inside she makes herself as invisible as a black cat in a coalhouse. I call her out and wait patiently for her to obey the summons, but she waits to see how long my patience will last, and I tell her she will be locked up for a long time if she refuses to come out. The thing is, I am not always certain she hasn't streaked out again. I could very well be talking to myself, and she knows I am not sure about whether I am or not. This morning I came to the conclusion she had darted out, and I locked the door. We were shopping in the middle of the morning when my wife asked me if I remembered seeing Topsy before we left home. I remembered talking to myself at the potting shed door, and I knew where she must have been when we departed. "I fear she is locked in the potting shed again," I said.

Well, it was mid-morning, and there have been times when it was the middle of the night and I came to the conclusion that she was imprisoned. I confess to being soft-centred and getting up out of my warm bed in the night to plod out in my dressing gown and unlock the potting shed door. I also confess to having done so only to find Topsy tripping along with me to find out why I was going to unlock the shed at such an ungodly hour. Once I even plodded all the way up to the shed above the little orchard and opened the door of that place and called her. She was outside. She had been having a great time hunting for mice. She accompanied me down to the cottage and then wandered away, wondering, I suppose, if I was sleep-walking or just becoming more and more eccentric in my old age.

I am thinking of writing a book like B.B.'s *Confessions of a Carp Fisherman*. Mine would be *Confessions of a Cat-Keeping Clown*.

A CAT CALLED TOPSY

IT would be nice if I could answer everyone who wrote to give advice on moving a cat from its hunting grounds. It is impossible. I thank them, each and every one, including that wonderful performer with animals, Johnny Morris. Johnny tells me that over 20 years ago he jokingly established the West of England Anthropomorphic Society to counteract some of the scientific arrogance prevailing in a certain Natural History Unit. I am afraid there is a general arrogance towards animals from people who hold there is no real evidence that animals work anything out, except as a result of appetite. Animals may be conditioned to do certain things.

Perhaps I am arrogant in claiming to have a rapport with most animals, because I always approach them with sympathy and understanding, as I am sure Johnny Morris does. But to give the consensus on cat moving, it seems to be generally agreed that the animal must be kept away from the upheaval caused by removal men as they clear rooms. At the other end it must have old and familiar things installed in its new surroundings. Some people advocate a tranquillising pill for the journey, and some are against doping a cat. Give her her favourite food and let her have her fill of it on arrival, they say. Johnny Morris says when he moves his cat, the move is made with the cat sitting on his wife's lap. It is a test of endurance, and the cat sticks it out because he trusts his owners. "It's no use saying try not to worry," he concludes, "for I get quite ill with worry when the awful day comes."

THERE is considerable satisfaction in the discovery that one is not alone in allowing an animal to almost dominate one's life. I was amused to hear how a friend who was similarly affected through his concern and affection for cats finally had to face the fact that if things went much further his livelihood might be endangered. A line has to be drawn somewhere, and some people would draw the line at having more than one cat, as I did, firmly believing that the cat I had was a one-off and there was no other cat in the world like her. My friend had a broader viewpoint, and three cats, one of them a highly intelligent and very friendly Siamese.

He also had an haute-cuisine restaurant with customers who were fascinated by the antics of the Siamese. The clever cat became one of the novelties of the place. Everyone petted him and gave him titbits he loved – morsels of fish, scampi, steak Diane, chicken Kiev and marinated game. Alas, the high life went to the poor cat's head in the end, although what happened was probably a blessing that saved him from stomach trouble. He began to help himself to the bon bouche before his fans had time to lift their forks, bolting down their slivers of veal and frog legs in a very uncivilised way. His owner had to harden his heart and banish his star attraction. Now a "hived off" Siamese languishes on cat food that eight out of ten cats prefer in a place several miles away. Too much was expected of that intelligent creature. Bringing it all down to simple fact, he was perhaps only an intelligent cat taking advantage of not so intelligent people.

A CAT CALLED TOPSY

HAVING time, at last, to look back on the traumas of moving from a place in which we had lived for 40 years, 25 of them at the cottage, I admit that the things we worried about didn't happen and those we discounted did. The removal men packed us up on the day before we moved, and that didn't bother Topsy a bit.

Our removal plans had been steadily centring on how Topsy would cope with it all, but Topsy tended to ignore the packers, although she inspected the corners they emptied to make sure one of her mice, escaped from her clutches on some past occasion, wasn't lurking in the back of a cupboard. The packers came and went. We didn't sleep very well that night because in the morning it was all going to happen. The movers-out would move in to begin to load a vast pantechnicon they had left outside overnight, and we would be off down to the vet to get poor Topsy tranquilised.

There was some doubt about the timing. If Topsy demanded to be let out at five to reconnoitre her mousing territory, she might not come back in time. As it turned out she did insist on early rising and trotted off into the half-light at five. I thought she might be difficult and stay out until 11 or 12, but she came back in two hours.

When the removal men arrived we popped her into a travelling basket and bade the cottage farewell, leaving a friend to hand over the keys. After being told how wild and ferocious Topsy could be, the vet opted for an injection instead of a pill. To our surprise, Topsy took the needle without complaint, and dozed all the way south. We carried her indoors when we arrived, and put her in a safe place while we struggled with furniture the builders had left piled in mountains.

In the morning, just before the removal men arrived, the postwoman came, and it seemed Topsy must have slipped out, for I couldn't find her anywhere in our muddle of furniture and knick-knackery. Horror-struck, I searched the house from top to bottom, and went outside and began calling her, all to no avail. Wherever she was, she paid no heed. The removers came and commiserated with me. My wife and I walked about in a daze and then, in the middle of the confusion, Topsy walked out of a room I couldn't have searched thoroughly. I had already raised the alarm.

News that Topsy, of *Country Life* fame, was lost, had travelled with the postwoman. A dear lady telephoned to say Topsy was on her birdtable, eating the food she had put out for the birds. She didn't want to scare her away by letting her dogs out for their morning airing until I got there. I had had a stiff drink by this time to restore my nerve, and thanked the caller. Topsy was beside me on the bed, the only place where either of us could rest in peace for a moment. After this, we were careful not to let her out of our sight for more than a minute, but it was several days before she would go beyond the threshold. Cats are much more concerned with people than territory, someone had already told me. They were quite right.

A CAT CALLED TOPSY

YESTERDAY the world came right for Topsy, and she went out to bask in the sun, sit with her eyes half-closed in the green leaves of the hedge-bottom and scale the far-up branches of the old apple trees to prove she isn't afraid of heights. Before this, she seemed withdrawn, much more highly strung than she used to be, and badly affected by the trauma of moving. More often than not, when she was ushered out through the back door, she lurked there to dash back indoors again. She seemed to see things we couldn't see. Her tail was nearly always standing out like a bottle brush, and she was jumpy. Worse than this, she had become unhouse-trained or so confused that she didn't know what she was doing half the time.

I began to think that she had become neurotic about the outside world. She would never run away but would run under the furniture and sit there, not at all herself. Shock, we told ourselves, so bad she couldn't think what a litter tray was about, but then, why should she when she had never been required to use one? I had come to think she was hallucinating when she peered round the door and retreated. Horses shy at things they imagine as much as things that shock them by physical impact. Dogs, too, have their invisible demons to contend with. Poor Topsy must have seen phantoms passing in the half-light, and after all the upheaval here, the clatter and bashing of removal men, carpet layers and flooring specialists, her nerves must have been in a very bad state. Like most animals, however, cats seem to have

remarkable powers of recovery. Gradually the high tension abated. Topsy went out and in, and stayed out longer. Now, I am happy to say, she is herself again. Like us she has finally settled. I might have expected all this to happen, but I didn't. I learn more about cats every day.

A CAT CALLED TOPSY

WE have become accustomed to the bats flitting about the bedroom gable immediately above the long window. On hot nights, and indeed even when it has been quite cool, we have kept the windows open. Topsy, who affects to retire with us, remains a nocturnal creature and will sit on the windowsill for hours, taking the breeze and watching the activity of the bats. Both species may be nocturnal, but their paths hardly ever cross since bats fly well above the ground, and cats can't fly. The fact that she can't hope to intercept a bat by a sudden pounce or a stroke of her well-taloned paw has not deterred Topsy from studying the problem. Her round black head with ears cocked is visible when I lie in bed, and I have seen the way it follows the outlines of the fast in-and-outing of the bats. One might suppose that long study of their ways and the problems involved in catching one of them would convince even the most dedicated of hunters that bats are beyond her, but Topsy is like an angler who won't give up on a wily trout that rises again and again in the same pool. Foolish cat, I call her, but I know what it is about.

Patience has at last been rewarded, for the other night Topsy caught her bat. It had been quite a day for the black huntress. In the morning she had been found on the mat in the hall, her teeth firmly set in the neck of an unfortunate squirrel, which was brought to me to let me see what a monstrously clever cat we harbour. By the time I was out lying in the sun, refreshing myself after a stint of mowing, the whole thing had faded from the cat-mind.

Topsy came past, heading for the jungle beyond the lawn, without giving us a second glance, and half an hour later trotted back with a large vole which she ate out in the open.

Come nightfall, she was on her usual perch by the window and I was too tired to watch her watching the bats, but I was not to be allowed to slumber undisturbed, for my wife presently shook me to say she thought we had a bat in the bedroom. Shades of Dracula! I could see Topsy silhouetted against the window, and she seemed to be watching things inside the bedroom rather than outside. I put the light on. The bat flew like a projectile against the lampshade and crashed to the floor. Topsy dropped from the sill, and in a moment she had the poor bat in her jaws. I jumped out of bed and rescued it and tossed it out of the window. Topsy resumed her vigil. My wife brought her head from under the bed clothes, and I got back into bed. This, so far as Topsy was concerned, was the end of a perfect day.

I recount what happened in response to a "telegram" from Aldeburgh in the laconic style of an age when an extra word cost another halfpenny. The wire was forwarded through *Country Life*, but I could hardly blame the editor if he had held on to it. It was dated 1983, but the form was a genuine antique, 12 words for sixpence, with every word telegraphed charged for, whether in address or text. It read: "What's happened to Topsy." I can't telegraph a reply, and the foregoing will have to serve.

A CAT CALLED TOPSY

CATS are notoriously creatures that love comfort and know where it is to be found. Topsy demonstrates this every day when she comes in and beats me to my chair just as I am about to sit myself down with the newspaper. She knows, too, that I haven't the heart to turn her out of it, so I sit on a hard seat in the kitchen while she settles in comfort to have her cat dreams. A cat is only a cat, some people would say, and their cat would be swiftly dislodged and taught its proper place, but I am not like that. I see the other person's point of view, and Topsy, so far as I am concerned, is a person, one of the family. The truth is that you are either a cat worshipper or you are not, and it helps if you not only adore cats but have a sense of the artistic. Cats are perfect models. They arrange themselves, body, legs, paws, so perfectly and yet so casually on the counterpane or carpet. Half their waking time is spent grooming. They groom when they have risen from the carpet and stretched. They groom when they have eaten and when they come in from the cold. When it rains and Topsy hesitates to go out, we apologise for the weather. We welcome her back and commiserate with her on her wet coat, forgetting that it is, like mink, entirely waterproof.

This is all absurd, I tell myself. An intelligent person wouldn't put up with it, but didn't the Egyptians, a civilised race, worship cats? And isn't there something very special about Topsy the green-eyed goddess who sits upright with her tail neatly arranged round her forefeet, looking for all the world like a pagan idol?

A CAT CALLED TOPSY

WHEN I was a boy, I was taught to talk to animals as though they understood what one said to them. Whether animals do or not, there is no harm in a one-sided conversation. Each day when I go to the paddock I am greeted by Raz and Pickles, my neighbour's ponies. Pickles will walk half a pace behind me and nudge me along, reminding me that if I have an apple about me, he is ready to munch one. I talk over my shoulder. Raz plods in front to get in the way as I near the far gate. I talk to her, too, for she gets jealous if I confine my remarks to the smaller pony. All this talk carries across the field, and is heard by Topsy. Topsy, like Raz, can't bear to be ignored, and she comes galloping across the field to complain.

From here on my remarks are addressed, not to the ponies, but to her. Her tail goes up and curls over at the tip. She is happy. The ponies no longer exist. We are off for a walk together. I pass out of the little paddock to the rough field beyond, and Topsy turns aside, slides into the undergrowth and proceeds on safari.

I wander about, do what I have come to do, and go back to the little paddock to cross to the gate and the lawn beyond. The ponies amble to accompany me across the paddock. I talk to them again, and Topsy materialises from the pine copse and hurries to get in line. We reach the gate with Topsy basking in my admiration. I come to the lawn and she deserts me.

WHILE I was out on the lawn looking again at the fallen tree, and pondering how to clear the brushwood and lighter branches, Topsy came to join me. The birch, rising from the rockery mound at one end, presented an incline to the broken stump, and Topsy ran up the trunk. I could imagine her telling me all that I would need to do as she paused and looked at me on her way to the stump. This branch would certainly have to be cut in three or four places with the chainsaw, and the lesser ones might be lopped. She went on with her survey until she was perched on the very end of the stump. I praised her on her findings, and she turned her tail into a hook to show that she too was pleased, but then she turned and stared up the path through the old fruit garden, for something up there had alarmed her.

A moment later I was astonished to see a pair of sleek black labradors working the ground and three people with them. Topsy sprang down from the tree and streaked across the grass to the back door. I knew that in a matter of minutes she would be upstairs under the bed. To say she is highly-strung is an under-statement. Even a caller at the door is enough to make her run for cover. Poor Topsy, she didn't show face again until the late afternoon. The invaders were from the nearby estate going through to drive pheasants back before a shoot. I didn't mind them doing this, but expected to have been told they were coming. I could hardly tell them my anxiety was for my cat's sanity.

A CAT CALLED TOPSY

TOPSY dashes out through the back door, almost tripping me in her haste to be there and accompany me on a walk across the lawn, and I call her to heel, knowing she will do exactly what she likes. We walk up to the far end, Topsy keeping abreast of me, but going her own way nevertheless. I am privileged to be keeping her company by this time. She isn't being taken for a walk now, but taking me. She races through the gateway into what used to be the fruit garden and slows to a trot, without looking back, but no doubt listening to make sure I am still following. She has that idle kind of mind that is diverted by the slightest thing, and stops to stare at the hedge beyond the path.

Her tail changes from a reasonably well-groomed appendage until it looks like a bottle brush. She has scented or seen something in the hedge, or the field beyond, something I haven't seen or scented. I call to her and she ignores me, the way an adult ignores a child when something important and beyond its comprehension comes up.

I pause and stare at the hedge. Could a fox or even a badger be skulking in the brushwood, or is Topsy hallucinating the way a cat we used to have would do, particularly when she had been eating the wrong things, like a morsel of dead jackdaw? The explanation remains unrevealed.

A CAT CALLED TOPSY

IT can hardly be denied that, despite countless generations of civilising, most cats remain nocturnal creatures. Putting out the cat is a ritual at least half of the cat-owners of this country religiously observe. Some keep the cat outdoors, and it doesn't really belong to them at all.

There are occasions when I think we belong to our cat and she doesn't really belong to us, but we can claim to have changed her from a nocturnal creature to a diurnal one. She sleeps in. To preserve this change in habit we go to great lengths to accommodate Topsy when she wants to go out, opening the door and waiting upon her return when it suits her idle mind to come back late on a cold night, or when she decides, at 5 am or so, to sally forth and test the moring air. A cat must be allowed to be a cat, albeit under a diurnal regime.

Topsy never stays out all night, except when, as happened one night last week, she gets carried away by the warmth of the long day, the perfume of honeysuckle, the rustlings in the grass and the twittering of birds that think dawn is about to come even if the clock has just chimed midnight. Topsy went out and didn't come back, though the door and the window were left open for her. I stood around for half an hour and rattled the door handle and clapped my hands. I finally retired to bed, but in case some intruder thought to explore the lower part of the house while I dozed, I closed the window and turned the key in the door. Sleeping fitfully, I occasionally thought I could hear Topsy mewing. I also thought of the fox carrying her off to the wood, and went down to do more door-knob rattling and hand-clapping.

No black creature came slowly across the airing green or materialised purring from the log shed. Where could she be? I gathered my dressing gown about me and walked round the outside of the house, my slippers getting wet with dew in the process. It was 3 am. There were no responses to my call. I visited her still-hunting perches and her dozing places in the long grass, but she was nowhere to be found. I told my wife at 5 am that I thought something might have happened to her. I was having a delayed three o'clock fit of depression that stayed with me until seven, when Topsy came casually across the green, brushing herself against my legs and going in for breakfast. I could have murdered her, but I am afraid I made a fool of myself and petted her instead.

A CAT CALLED TOPSY

HOW fine the line is when it is a question of a hunter getting his dinner or his prey surviving. I watched Topsy watching the squirrel out on the lawn. She had no chance of dashing at it and catching it before it got to the birch stump. She knew it couldn't be done. So did the squirrel, but then the squirrel became less vigilant and more occupied with what he was about, and Topsy was able to move ten yards nearer, sitting in exactly the same, patient crouch. If the squirrel took in what she had done, he didn't show it. His inbuilt defence mechanism registered a cat in the same posture as before. He didn't seem to have recorded a reduction in the range.

The squirrel went on boring his little holes and fussing about until the lethal distance was reached. It depended now on how fast he could go and how quick off the mark Topsy was. When she finally triggered her spring, the squirrel almost jumped out of his skin, but he was away, scuttling over the short grass for dear life. For a moment he seemed about to meet his doom. Topsy was a foot behind when he hit the tree-trunk and clawed his way up the rough bark.

She made no attempt to rush after him. Fast though she may be running up a tree-trunk, she was up against the fastest thing in its own element. She stared up at the squirrel jumping through branches and passing on to another tree. I knew what was going on in her mind: next time, with any luck, there would be a different scenario and she would have squirrel for dinner.

One would need to be a qualified student of animal behaviour to look dispassionately on the things that some animals do without being anthropomorphic. It is natural for humans to attribute what other animals do to reason and intelligence. I chose, perhaps, to think that my grandfather's dog mourned. The scientifically-minded person would put in another way. The dog missed attention. Part of its life-support system had been damaged. My cat rubs round my feet because she likes the contact. She also likes a titbit from my supper tray, and cats are damned as cupboard-lovers. Dogs are equally guilty. We can boil down everything in the relationship to physical or psychological need. We make our choice and persuade ourselves that our cat is loving and not made dependent. Food becomes secondary. Creature comfort is discounted, even when it is obvious that the cat is hanging around to steal our warm chair the minute we get out of it.

I am afraid I choose to delude myself. I need to believe that there is something more to it than cupboard love. She picks on me because I am a special person. I won't have it any other way, though in my less besotted moments I admit to myself that anyone who would devote themselves to Topsy as I have done, would earn the same place in her affection. She is, when all is said and done, a cat. A dog is a dog. What more can be said? We read what we wish to read into any account of animal behaviour.

MY COUNTRY GARDEN

Perhaps the farmer in me made me more interested in growing fruit and vegetables than in cultivating flowers. When we lived in Wales, I had to buy myself a mad little bouncing cultivator, which was the only thing that could turn the surface of the steep slope of the old kitchen garden. I grew some fine cabbages and beans there, and enough potatoes to last a year. I left part of the slope in grass and planted fruit trees. The sheep I got to crop the grass barked the trees so they had to go.

My wife does the real gardening, tending her flower beds with loving care; my role is really that of labourer and park-keeper. We have six acres here, almost two acres more than we had in Wales, and I make mountains of grass cuttings without ever succeeding in cutting all the grass down. The soil, a sullen, greasy clay above flint and chalk, does not help – although it does wonders for rhododendrons and azaleas. I cultivate a few gooseberry and raspberry bushes and recently built myself a greenhouse.

I hold the wilderness in check with a certain satisfaction. I would have made a good pioneer, carving a clearing in the bush and building a homestead, but I settle for the home-grown wilderness here and watch the thistledown rising on the summer breeze.

MY COUNTRY GARDEN

IT has been quite a day, with 14 sheep penned not five yards from the kitchen window and kept closely confined there, waiting for their owner to come and take them away before they get a chance to knock more apples from the trees or overturn the beehives. A succession of policemen came to answer my request for assistance in tracing the owner of the flock. The first one threw himself headlong on the ground without being able to catch the sheep he aimed at, and then caught a lamb which, as one might have expected, bore no ear-mark. The second policeman arrived to look into a message that had been passed on to him from his headquarters, and hot on his heels came his sergeant and another constable. With so much help I was sure that I would soon be relieved of the burden, and meet the man whose invading flock had forced me to get out of bed at half-past six in the morning, and go away up to our back wall, rebuilding the stones and applying a few hanks of barbed wire to our crumbling fortifications up there.

AT the moment, now that the June drop is past, it seems as though we might have a fair crop of apples, although one tree didn't blossom for the first time in 12 years. The plum tree, which has given us good crops for about five years, had little blossom. What there was either wasn't pollinated, because the bees were reluctant to go out in the cold days of early spring, or suffered from the depredations of the bullfinches. The bullfinch has a distinct preference for plum blossom, I think. The small florets are taken to pieces with a confetti effect which, some people say, is why the bullfinches destroy the blossom. One sees and hears bullfinches at blossom time, but they are not so readily spotted in high summer, nor are their nests easily found during the breeding season. We shall miss our Victoria plums, which have hitherto been eaten ripe, put into pies and flans or bagged up for the deep freeze when the stones have been removed. We have become resigned to diminishing returns with soft fruit, and gooseberries don't do well on the light sandy soil at the top of what was once the kitchen garden. The blackcurrant bushes should have been renewed, but the tedium of picking and preparing blackcurrants dulled my enthusiasm for cultivating them. On the other hand, I can bear with raspberry picking, and love nothing better than a raspberry tart or raspberries in cream. In previous years the bees got credit for the abundance of the crop. This year, looking back, I think the seal was set on everything when we had such inhospitable weather in March and April.

MY COUNTRY GARDEN

NOT everyone can plant a tree. Few of us have gardens large enough to accommodate trees, and a great many people have no gardens at all. In the cause of conservation it behoves those who have room for trees to plant one or two, if not for their own sake, at least for the sake of others. When a friend rang me up and asked me if I would like some seedling trees I thought about it for a moment. I am surrounded by trees. There is a tree order on my wood, in the interest of local amenity, and not directly the conservation of natural resources.

I asked what kind of trees I was being offered and was told they were Norway spruce. I have ample room, but six conifers will be more than enough, even though the spruce will be a pleasant thing to look at as a change from the Austrian pines which dominate the cottage and its surroundings.

Schoolchildren are being encouraged to persuade their parents to plant trees, and seedlings are being sold at about 12 pence each. The majority of the trees planted this year will inevitably turn out to be conifers. Conifers are easier to plant. They aren't stopped or stunted by being moved, and their root structure actually benefits by transplant; but how I wish we could forego the easy way and plant beech and oak or even ash. Planting this sort of tree is an act of faith. It has no short-term benefit, even for the young man who may put in a spruce and see it topping his roof well within his lifetime. I will put in the Norway spruce, but I have also done something this week which I feel is a step forward. I have gone in search of the naturally-seeded pines which in the past 10 to 15 years have found places in the jungle that clothes the cliff, and have cleared spaces round them to give them light and air. There is no better tree than one that has proved itself strong enough to come up through the brambles and thorn bushes. Once its top is above the undergrowth it shoots up.

Two young trees I discovered were nearly four feet in height. I was delighted at finding them. Now they will have a little more sun and air. I am sure that in the year of the tree they will put on better growth, but the endless carpet of conifers is to me a ritual sort of forestry. It is time to impose a quota of hardwood planting on this widespread enterprise, curtailing funds, perhaps, if the quota is not reached, or making special grants for hardwood planting if there is no other way.

MY COUNTRY GARDEN

THE caterpillar of the cabbage butterfly, which is certainly the best-known of British butterflies and the most widespread of the whites, generally seems to pupate where it can attach itself to the underside of some piece of dry wood such as the timber of a shed. There it hangs, like a curd of fat from a cheese vat, until it is ready to emerge as a butterfly in April or May according to the weather in spring. It is a minor miracle or witch's curse, the emergence of this buoyant, white insect that flies so erratically from place to place. I am inclined to think of it as a curse rather than a poet's inspiration, for the cabbage butterfly lingered and laid more eggs in a few seconds than my birds did in the whole of autumn. The Brussels sprouts plants were devastated by the browsing caterpillars. I picked caterpillars off into jars and transported the catch to the hens. The bantams showed no great interest and only the pheasants seemed to recognise the fat swarming mass as something good to eat.

Now I find pupae here and there in sheltered corners. A natural instinct for places safe from frost and freezing rain guides the over-fed caterpillar to the place in which it will live as a pupa, but I can't help wondering where all those caterpillars went. I picked my share. The birds picked twice as many, but even so a great many caterpillars must have survived. We shall see in the spring. Things are so well ordered in the insect-parasite world that the butterfly comes out just when the spring cabbages are fit for the table or when young plants have been hardened off.

I remember long ago when I was at school finding pupae on the timbers of a garden shed at my grandfather's and bringing these back home to see the butterflies emerge in spring. My father happened along just when I was happily releasing the newly-emerged butterflies through the window into his garden. They clustered and mated on his cabbage plants, and I am afraid he took a very discouraging view of my little experiment. We had never had any shortage of cabbage butterflies. The whole thing was downright irresponsibility on my part, he said, and I took the blame for the ravages inflicted on our cabbage patch for more than a year afterwards.

MY COUNTRY GARDEN

March 1975

IN order to discover more about butterflies I have been checking up on the plants upon which the different species depend. Basically the stock of any species of butterfly depends upon the food of the caterpillar – the host plant upon which the female deposits her eggs. One could conceivably think because a particular butterfly regularly appeared in the garden at a certain time in the year, the species had bred in the immediate locality, but the butterfly might be in passage, a rare migrant, or part of a movement of butterflies annually affected by a prevailing wind. On the other hand, discovering the caterpillar and a wealth of food upon which it might browse, one could reasonably assume that it was local and perhaps a native of one's own patch of ground.

The fact that we have more than our share of strong, healthy nettles probably has something to do with the butterflies we see in mid-summer and towards autumn. At these times we get more than our share of red admirals, peacocks and tortoiseshells. The food of a great many of our native butterflies is the common nettle. Thistles might feed the larvae of the rare painted lady. The white admiral's caterpillar feeds on honeysuckle, the purple emperor on willow and sallow. The speckled wood is addicted to couch grass. We have both the grass and the butterfly here. Other sorts depend upon grasses, as one would expect from butterflies with names like the gatekeeper, the large heath, the meadow brown. The wall brown's caterpillar feeds on bog cotton or weaves itself a bower in it. The comma feeds not only on nettle, but will be found on willow and hop. The beautiful fritillaries, as one might expect, have a taste for violets. What happens to them all in wintertime? The chrysalis hangs in some sheltered place, protected from the wind and the cold, or lies buried in dead vegetation until the time comes for the butterfly to emerge and breed again.

MY COUNTRY GARDEN

March 1975

ITAKE a childish delight in bonfires and some- times find myself becoming enslaved by the lighting of a fire in the garden. A few dry twigs and perhaps a broken seed box or other piece of gardening debris will encourage me to feel in my pocket for the matches. A couple of handfuls of crisp, dry leaves and the ensuing whiff of smoke are all it takes to get me hurrying about to keep the thing going. I become drugged by the scents, transfixed by the screen of glowing sparks sup- ported by the breeze. When the fire threatens to die I look about for another pile of leaves blown into a corner, another dry, bone-like branch lean- ing against the limestone wall. The thing goes on and on, and I find more and more items to burn.

A few weeks ago I got caught up in it all again and devoted an afternoon to what I called a tidying-up operation. I burned old nesting boxes and a sledge with which the children had had a lot of fun 20 years ago, but of course I didn't mention that it all began when I walked through a carpet of walnut leaves as crisp as breakfast cereal. I couldn't resist raking the carpet into a heap and putting a match to it. After that I was incapable of letting the thing go out. Tidying up was a by-product. I was temp- ted to carry on next day when I saw grey ash rising in a column when the breeze picked it up, but there wasn't a thing in sight to burn. A dead fire is unexciting to a pyromaniac, if that is what I am. Before I could extend my search for kindling a fine rain fell. There is nothing more frustrating to the addict than burning wet sticks or damp leaves.

September 1975

THE hot summer must have suited the wal- nut tree, for the crop is outstanding. I have never seen so many clusters of walnuts, not that I will do anything with them, mind you. The business of beating walnut trees is too much for me when I have so many other calls on my time. In the middle of the heatwave some relatives came and admired the walnuts and I suggested that they might like to pickle a few. The clusters within reach were easily gathered and they soon had all they wanted. The grey squirrels, like the birds settling on the fruit trees, needed moisture in one form or another I suppose, for they nibbled at some of the green walnuts. The birds pecked at the green apples as they always do when there is a shortage of water. Drought and hot weather may have suited the walnut, but it did nothing for the vegetable garden. Beetroot bolted and beans tended to set only on the top of the vine. The swedes didn't swell until we had the big downpour.

It is all over now and we are back to the mixed weather the forecasters like because they are bound to be right most of the time. It should produce a good crop of blackberries if nothing else. A very wet grey squirrel – they look really rat-like when their brush has been through a downpour – is busy chopping off the walnuts at this minute. They fall on the ground beneath and the squirrel ignores them. I suppose there is some purpose in what the destructive little fellow is up to, but it escapes me. Perhaps he is only getting his hand in for the gathering of nuts squirrels are supposed to indulge in with such industry later on.

MY COUNTRY GARDEN

January 1976

A READER writes: "Your paragraph on inkcaps prompts me to report that last autumn three of them actually grew through the asphalt at the bottom of my drive. One is quite used to seeing seedlings doing this but I have never before seen a fungus achieve it. Incidentally, it is not the ordinary shaggy inkcap *Coprinus comatus*, which causes nausea when eaten in combination with alcohol, but its relative *Coprinus atramentarius*, which is less common and easily recognised."

One tends to think of the growth of a fungus as being something plastic, like the flow of resin or tree sap, and not at all akin to the germinative force exerted by a seed sprouting under a paving stone. It may be that a comparatively thin layer of asphalt offered little resistance to the fungus which emerged through small cracks in the material. I remember finding a giant puffball on the wall of the vinery before we knocked it down.

The fungus appeared to have developed on the surface of the concrete, but when I removed it I found it had come through the tiniest hole into which I suppose the spore must have settled a year or two before. Spores from fungus become airborne, drift and settle in the same way as windborne seeds. A fertile crevice or crack in material warmed by the sun would encourage growth, like a rosebed on which dandelion or thistle seeds have settled.

June 1976

THIS will surely go down as the year of the ladybird in our part of the world. I suppose the present super-abundance of them has something to do with the sort of summer we had last year when greenfly were a plague. The sort we have are two-spotted which are more common than the seven-spotted variety at the moment. The brilliant red of the tiny beetle is like a jewel on the young nettles – and both are everywhere in spring.

I wondered how beetles such as these could remain so plentiful when there are thrushes and blackbirds nesting and free-range hens and bantams all over the place, but the book tells me ladybirds have built-in protection in the form of bitter fluid exuded from the leg joints, and this is distasteful to would-be predators, which is just as well. Nothing counteracts the greenfly better than the ladybird, and they need to be counteracted while ants are so busy fostering them on every plant.

MY COUNTRY GARDEN

FOR the first time in years I have planted a row of potatoes. Years ago we always grew enough to see us through the year, but then I began to find other crops more profitable so far as the kitchen was concerned and grew no potatoes at all. Soon we gave up eating them. Too much starch is bad for the waistline anyway and there would be no need for drastic slimming diets if people would only give up things like potatoes, bread, sweet biscuits and sugar. Now a longing for a freshly dug potato has prompted me to plant a single row. There is a touch of nostalgia about it.

I recall the wonderful flavour of the potatoes dug from the garden when I was a child, potatoes with a nutty taste, potatoes that broke open as they were spooned on to the plate and really needed to be eaten with nothing but salty farm butter to make them perfect. No one bought potatoes and no one would have dreamed of digging them before they were demanded in the kitchen, at least while the summer lasted. Charles Lamb might have written another dissertation on the potato, I always felt, or had just one or two with the roast suckling pig.

WORD had come to me that our eastern defences had been breached. The invading hordes would soon come pouring in unless I went up there without delay and made good the damage. Having no stock of land-mines to hand, and being equally discouraged by the law regarding mantraps, I had to be content with several hanks of wire and some angle iron with which I might reinforce the wall. I find that a sort of Western Front entanglement of wire loosely hung stops the invasion but, of course, does nothing to discourage the rock roller.

My bits of angle iron and wire needed to be supplemented by a heavy hammer, wire-cutters, gloves etc, all of which I had to elevate from 100 feet in less than 300 yards. I was quite out of breath by the time I had got all the stuff to the south-east corner, where I began rebuilding the wall and rigging up the wire. The danger was that anything I dropped would immediately begin to roll downhill at increasing speed until it fell over a minor precipice into the wood. This happened twice, but in the end I was satisfied and stood to admire the view. It was worth the effort of climbing the cliff just to be there and have a hawk sweep past my head, and to watch the world of ants away down in the town where they were making traffic queues to the supermarket car park. One needs to get perspective on the world every now and again, and I enjoy high places that let me look down at farms and gardens and smoking chimneypots. I stood on the rocky ledge for much longer than it had taken me to repair the wall.

MY COUNTRY GARDEN

A FRIEND who lives in America remarks in a letter that he has just returned from an outing to collect morels for his supper. Mushroom hunters, he adds, don't tell even their best friends where they find their mushrooms, and I suppose this is part of the reason why I have only once come upon the morel. I know one copse where once in a while, a morel might be found, but in this part of the world I must admit they are probably as hard to come by as truffles. We have to be content with the occasional blusher, the puffball, inkcap, the field mushroom or horse mushroom. The spring climate here is too briefly suitable for wild-mushroom growth, I think. In autumn the more even temperature in which fungi may develop tends to continue for longer, although once there is a touch of frost all the delicate sorts stop completely, even in sheltered places.

A time was when I had a tucked-away mental map of places where I could gather a bag of mushrooms without having to be up with the lark and hurrying across fields, looking over my shoulder to see whether I was being dogged by someone else or not. But the map is out of date now and I think new methods of cultivation and livestock rearing have changed the nature of the ground on which mushrooms once grew. The morel I found in the copse looked too beautiful to pick, but I thought of it a few days older with the fly on it or wilting in a cooler climate, and picked it for my supper. Even this effort was wasted, for something intervened to make me forget about its presence in my game-bag until it had shrunk and liquefied.

September 1977

ANOTHER generation will talk of the year of the great drought and how unnerving it became when the sun blazed down for days on end and the undergrowth became like dry tinder. I remember my grandparents talking of the year of the big snow, although I am not exactly sure when that was, and the year of the short corn, which seems now to have been a year of water shortage. Once, when these disasters were being gone over, I remember being reprimanded for asking about the year when the potatoes didn't grow because none were planted. It didn't do to joke about human suffering. There had been a potato famine in great-grandfather's time.

The consequence of the year of drought, 1976, might be recorded on both sides of the ledger, profit-and-loss, in the great resurgence of flowers in the spring when we never had finer daffodils and snowdrops, the wonderful roses of summer and the fine strawberry crop. The debit side is our total lack of fruit on apple and pear trees. In the year of the drought we stored enough apples to see us right through to the following April, but we have none to store and none to pick. In the year of the drought we lost two apple and one pear tree. The pear tree was in its old age and had deep roots. But I think the apple trees, which were by no means old, hadn't got a well-enough developed root structure to reach moisture slowly receding from them as the hot days continued. I am afraid I shall not live long enough to tell my great-grand-children of the year of drought and the year when blossom fell without fruit forming.

October 1977

THE blackberry season in upon us in this part of the world, where people make a great thing of gathering the berries along the roadside hedges and taking them home to put them in the deep freeze, unlike an older generation who would make blackberry jam of the harvest. Alas, pollution affects hedgerows along roads on which traffic is comparatively heavy, and there is reason to believe that a degree of poisoning may result from eating berries obtained from such situations. For my own part, I like to prospect the deeper countryside and pick a few berries to go with our stewed apple where petrol fumes and roadside sprays cannot contaminate the fruit.

On our own piece of ground we have more than our share of brambles, although the berries are of poor quality. Limestone tends to wash bare and the brambles grow in fissures where their nourishment is never very great. We do have, however, a variety of blackberries. I have identified at least three. Some are low-growing with quite big berries which the birds don't seem to eat. There are, I learn from Keble Martin's monumental work, close to 400 species of blackberry and, like some species of fly, a whole book could be devoted to them. I have tasted two or three blackberries including the cloud berry, which I remember picking on a patch of scrubland. The cloud berry is not black when ripe but amber-coloured. A sub-genus with a red berry grows on wet limestone, and the raspberry itself comes within the same general family group as the blackberry.

MY COUNTRY GARDEN

WHAT to do with an unexpected grape harvest, when I hadn't bothered to thin the bunches, suddenly became a problem when, as neglected grapes do, one or two showed signs of mildewing. Long ago my father used to complain that he was like that Biblical leader of the Israelites who needed someone to help keep his arms in the air while the battle was being won. Father tended his vines with great care and thinned according to the book. For a while I did this, but too often the crop was deprived of the last touch of the sun that produced the sugar, and I gave up the arm-straining business of using thinning scissors. This season it looked to me as though there would be more bunches than the vines could support, and the crop would be nothing but small, sour grapes. Then came the Indian summer, the only summer we have had, and I discovered the fine muscadines that taste so good when they are really ripe. One can toy with a few bunches of Alicante and those smaller green grapes after a meal or pick them and eat them in passing, but several dozen bunches all coming on at the same time we couldn't manage.

This morning I harvested two very large buckets of black and green grapes and carried them to the potting shed. The grapes may be what the customs man would accept as "of no commercial value" but they are much too good to put on the compost, or feed to the hens, supposing they would do the hens any good, which they probably wouldn't. Now I have to string the harvest, wash and prepare the grapes for the fermenter, gently crush them and add some yeast to get things going. After that the liquid has to be drained and bottled under airlocks for the proper process of wine-making to continue. It is all something of a chore when I hadn't thought to set up wine-making this year. The trouble with the cold-house grape is that it lags behind the grape grown in the heated vinery. Rarely, if ever, does it have the right sugar content to produce a good medium-sweet wine. I have sometimes in the past cheated a little and added some honey rather than sugar. Honey imparts a particular flavour of its own, but this year I have little to spare for the business. One thing about it all is that even without the natural sugar, there is still the distinctive flavour and delicate colour of the grapes so that the wine is much better than anything made from commercially produced grape juice. The fermenter will take five gallons. I expect to finish up with perhaps 20 litres, allowing for evaporation in the process. Two or three years from now I should have a fair stock of vintage '78.

MY COUNTRY GARDEN

WHERE have all the highly thought of, old varieties of potato gone, I wonder, as I lift the King Edwards I planted this year. Some were, of course, prone to scab, eelworm and blight. Some undoubtedly didn't please the man who grew them commercially and spent a lot of money irrigating and spraying potatoes over which the modern housewife showed no discrimination. A potato is a potato in a pre-pack and sometimes comes with the milk. All that stuff the older generation talked about the particular quality and flavour of the old potato would carry no weight in the day of instant mash, or starch granules, a thousand miles away from grandad's potato patch. I remember my elders going into raptures about waxy potatoes, potatoes that roasted like no other and potatoes that looked beautiful because they had red skins, blue skins or pale yellow skins. I suppose with the control of seed and the care taken to prevent disaster, which might leave us with an import deficit if the potato crop failed in Lancashire and the Fens through disease, a lot of the old-fashioned varieties must be almost unobtainable. In my part of the world I certainly never hear mention of Gladstone, Dunbar Standard or Kerr's Pink. The general purpose potato is King Edward, ripening after midsummer as the main crop does, and being an excellent potato boiled, roasted, mashed or done in its jacket. I wonder, nevertheless, if something as distinctive as the flavour of a russet apple hasn't been lost along the way. Could it be that somewhere, the connoisseur of the potato still cultivates the kind his father and grandfather swore by?

THE present glut of apples is not exactly reflected by a lowering of prices in the shop, but then perhaps only a Chancellor of the Exchequer would be so naïve as to imagine that such a thing could be. Glut we have, however; more apples than we could make into apple jelly or store in slices in deep freeze bags, more apples than would make all the apple pies a glutton for apples pies could ever want. What is to be done with them? I eat an apple a day. I have apple on my breakfast cereal, apple with my apple dumpling, apple with my after-dinner apple.

I went down and saw the grocer and got some more boxes to use in the apple store, which used to be the potting shed, but is now overpoweringly scented with ripening fruit. I could make apple wine and construct a cider press, but I care for neither drink very much.

I have already given apples away to all my friends, persuading them that they could try apple fritter, apple sauce or apple fool, if there is such a thing. I thumb through the recipe book and when the apple recipes are exhausted, think to substitute apple for all the other fruits used in cooking. The hens are eating apples. The old cock pheasant keeps his end up. Last year we hadn't an apple of any sort. I give thanks for the harvest, but Lord, this is ridiculous.

MY COUNTRY GARDEN

THE bleating of sheep at five o'clock in the morning brought me half out of the land of dreams, imagining I was back where I was 15 or more years ago when I kept sheep, first in the old orchard and then up in the newly planted apple trees on the slope that was once the kitchen garden. Sheep belong in my nightmares. While I played at flockmaster, without much help from a Cairn terrier, I ran myself into the ground and watched the sheep nibbling the bark from my young trees, ignoring the lush grass they were supposed to eat.

I am a little less agile now, and on my way downstairs to see what the sheep were up to it struck me that the problem wasn't mine this time. My sheep went over the hill more than a decade ago so this lot belonged to my neighbour, and they did. They were in the lane in front of the house, bundling to and fro, looking for a lush bite. Their own pasture was threadbare a month ago and now they are determined to find pastures new. We had just put a few bedding plants along the wall below our windows, and it seemed to me that the munching sheep would devour them all. I rushed out, whistling up an imaginary dog, and the flock went off like a herd of buffalo up the lane to the stile.

The stile has been badly vandalised these few months past. The sheep simply flowed over it, heading for the rough land up above the footpath. Anyone who knows the ways of sheep prospecting for better grazing knows they will return when they are driven off. I drove them back again before I made my early morning cup of coffee and then telephoned my neighbour to say that the sheep were crossing the stile. In the afternoon he and his brother arrived in a Land-Rover into which they had loaded bags of sand and cement as well as several milking pails of water. I went to watch them rebuild the stile and improve the defences. They worked very hard. It was a hot afternoon, and not one for lifting great rocks up on to a wall, but they achieved their purpose and finished the job in a most workmanlike fashion. So long as the cement got time to set hard before the vandals discovered what had been done, it would be alright.

The destruction of the stile had been easy when the mortar was old and crumbling. The vandals did return, I discovered, for they left initials in the hardening cement, but they didn't have the strength, or perhaps the time to take the stile to bits that evening. Everything was as firm as a rock the following morning. I hadn't the heart to telephone my neighbour to give him the news that the leading ewe, the one that had led the migration, was back on the other side of the stile this morning. I drove her back again. Her companions found the obstacle just too much for them. A ewe that can scramble up a five foot wall, ignoring the steps of the stone stile completely, is a formidable creature. Since the wall can't be made higher, two remedies are available. My neighbour can hobble his wayward ewe or resign himself to a month of mutton stew.

MY COUNTRY GARDEN

COMPLAINING about the English summer, which I suppose is not much different from the Scottish or Welsh summer, hasn't changed anything, but this year it has been one of the most variable I can remember, particularly here on the seaboard. The forecaster's map has hardly faded from the screen before things have changed and we are in a downpour instead of the sunshine they have just told us we have had.

The only blessing in a summer now running into autumn has been in the numbers of butterflies. I have never seen so many, and I put this down to the off-and-on nature of the weather, heavy rain and then sunshine. Where a butterfly goes in a downpour I have never stayed to find out, but the real point is that a good amount of rain on our limestone soil promotes a growth of nettles. Even the valerian with its roots knotted in the mortar of the limestone walls flourishes. Our butterflies love both.

In the course of my life I have only been able to spot about 16 of the species of butterfly to be encountered in Britain. A naturalist will record well over 50 native species or regular migrants, but I am not one who has gone in pursuit of the bright elusive butterfly. I have ticked off only what I have seen by chance, male or female of the species.

There may, of course, be some confusion for amateurs like myself in identifying one variety of, say, the gatekeeper from another, because variations there are. This week I have been delighted to tick off seven species of butterfly on my patch of ground, each carefully observed with the field glasses and the book in my free hand, something I haven't done with such care before. There was the large white. It didn't need much checking up on, and the peacock, like a black wedge of wood with its wings closed while it sat contemplatively on a valerian flower, wasn't too difficult to identify.

The comma was my greatest delight. It is, for me, one of the most beautiful of butterflies and compares with any fritillary. The speckled wood is commoner than even the large white. We are never without them. The orange tip haunts the area beyond the old sundial for some reason. I suppose its favourite plant is there somewhere.

The gatekeepers, both male and female, are a little more elusive. The small white pleases me, although it is probably only a lesser cabbage butterfly when it comes down to it. We have hardly any buddleia bushes now although we once had quite a number and these attracted other butterflies like the tortoiseshell and the red admiral which, with any luck, we may yet see.

MY COUNTRY GARDEN

A VARIETY of spiders have shown up in my garden these past few days to drape bushes with gossamer hammocks in which flies and other insects are entrapped. I must confess to ignorance of the different species of *araneidae*. I know the plughole spider that won't go away when the bath is flushed, and the money spider which old country people would whirl round their heads once or twice in the hope that it would increase their wealth. Small spiders come sliding down ropes like rock climbers descending, and others, with Tarzan-like ease, swing across the vast chasm of the path to the hens, rigging up a tightrope into which I walk in the morning.

All of these are just spiders to me because I lack all knowledge of entomology beyond half a dozen flies upon which trout regularly feed. The beauty of these autumn webs delights me, nevertheless, because on damp mornings they are hung with tiny jewels of moisture tracing a pattern as perfect as a honeycomb. There would seem to be a whole tribe of spiders living in the grass and the crevices of outdoor limestone walls, just as there are more urban, domestic spiders weaving webs in the dusty rafters of the potting shed.

This morning when I awoke, I couldn't see more than four or five yards for mist, and perhaps it was the humidity that suddenly made all those spiders get weaving. The cypressus was swathed in webs. Young seedling pines had been quickly mummified. I was puzzled about it until I remembered how, last evening, the midges were such a great nuisance, nibbling at one's wrists and ankles. Nature has a way of balancing things out, of course – more flies, more spiders, more spiders, more insectivorous birds eating. I noticed, not just the spiders, but the occasional fly struggling to escape from the web. What puzzles me is where they all come from, and where they go when the feast of flies is at an end. Perhaps, like many water-bred insects, they have an ephemeral life and, like the spiralling midges and flitting mosquitoes, they are gone in a matter of hours.

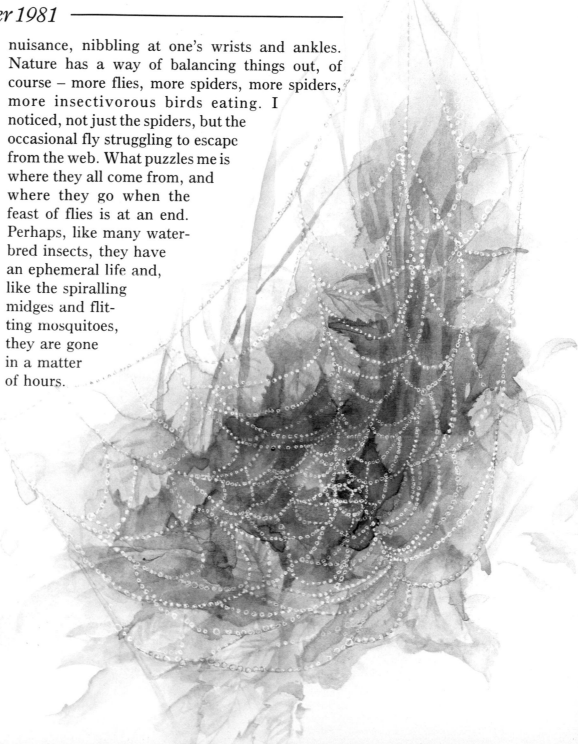

MY COUNTRY GARDEN

THE fierce wind as well as gales brought about the fall of the leaf. I always think the American "Fall" is a more appropriate name for the season. Autumn to me is when the leaves change colour, when first the sycamores, and then the beech, the oak and the ash, scorch, turn yellow and red and transform a world that has lost the shine of summer.

Our landscape is one of mixed deciduous trees and conifers. The broad-leaved trees have a tendency to become blanketed in limp, lifeless foliage. The conifers may be evergreen, but they too have a way of showing rust when the sap is going back in the deciduous trees and draining the life from their foliage. All this is cleared up, at least arboreally, when the gales come at the back end of the year. The deciduous trees are stripped. The dead needles on the pines are carried away. We at last find we can see the wood take on its winter look, even if the ground is covered in a slippery mass of yellowed leaves. It happens in a day or two, but it seems to have happened overnight when one morning a conifer stands out among the up-reaching, straggling branches of sycamore or ash, and the slope beneath the beech tree is covered by a newly rolled out carpet of curled red leaves. I watch the young bantams foraging among these leaves, busily scratching them aside with a movement rather like a skater trying to get along against a wind, and finding tiny items of food on the moist surface beneath. Sometimes I sweep up leaves and take them into one of the henhouses as litter, but dead leaves crumble to dust and are less suitable for this purpose than sawdust from my chainsaw labours.

In a week or two the wood took on its winter look, and it seems now as though summer was more than a year ago, for there was nothing memorable about it. It was just an interval between the breaking of the leaf and the fall, and to brighten my days I shall look for the tip of the very first snowdrop. I have seen this appear before Christmas although I have never written to *The Times* about it.

MY COUNTRY GARDEN

WHILE I always notice the way trees lose their leaves, one species after another as winter takes hold, I never manage to see how lesser plants like nettles defoliate and die back. All at once, where there was a barrier of dark green leaves, a nettle bed, there is a forest of dry stalks. I am quite fond of the nettle. I set store by it when I see the host of butterflies it can

encourage. I recall once having a dish of young nettle tips which tasted a bit like spinach. An aunt used to make nettle beer. Here in Wales old people would harvest nettles to make soup, and the habit continued long after the hungry '40s, for I know a man who remembers his mother sending him to gather them.

The five thousand could be fed here in the height of the season, but I have never been driven to making soup of the leaves. Once, however, when cortisone not withstanding, I had trouble with my elbow joints, I grasped the nettle and, using a bunch of them, flayed my arms. It did absolutely nothing for my condition. An enormous cortisone needle had proved no more effective. The trouble cleared of its own accord in a year. It was tennis elbow, and while it lasted I complained bitterly.

With the nettles now gone I feel I should get out there and cut down the stalks. I have quite a forest of them with, here and there, a tall, dead tree of cow parsnip or hog's weed. I was always told that nettles thrive in the richest soil, and this seems to be borne out by the fact that our best nettles grow at the bottom of the slope against the hedge. Erosion of the light soil on the slope causes richer material to accumulate at the hedge bottom. In the wood, nettles thrive on the sides of the path where humus is trodden in place by pedestrian traffic. There are liquid preparations to eliminate the nettle but here we should need thousands of gallons of the stuff, and cow parsnip and burdock would almost certainly take over.

MY COUNTRY GARDEN

THE wilderness beyond the small cultivated area here was once as well kept as a public garden. Now whatever used to be cultivated and still survives, struggles upwards through thorn and ivy, long grass and dog mercury. In the odd corner a herb, planted perhaps 100 years ago by a diligent gardener, flourishes and spreads as far as the undergrowth permits. I don't know very many of these herbs, but when my wife comes upon them she looks them up to find what culinary use they may have. My contribution to the herbal thing amounts to the propagation of a kind of mint that almost outdid the ivy encroaching on the old rose garden, and the planting of greater celandine and comfrey. The greater celandine is supposed to be good for warts, and I am thankful to say I had little or no use for it. Comfrey gives me backache, for it is as hard to dig out of the ground, once it is established, as horseradish. Culpeper's *Complete Herbal* has come to me a little late in the day as a gift from a friend, but I don't see celandine mentioned, although the lesser is. The great 17th-century herbalist was full of praise for comfrey, and passed on the information that Dioscorides claimed it would join meat together when "cut asunder" providing the meat was boiled in it. Excellent, he said, for "all wounds internal and external, and very good in the case of injury to the eyes".

I was delighted to have a life-long puzzle solved when I discovered elecampane. As a child I often heard my grandparents talking about a cure for a harsh cough, something called Alick O'Pain. I pondered this without ever asking and concluded that "Alick O'Pain" must have been one of our Irish harvesters whose stock remedy this substance was. Elecampane, the *Complete Herbal* tells us, was known to the Greeks and Romans as an agricultural plant, as a medicine and a condiment. It was cultivated in other countries for its medicinal properties, though not in Britain. W. Keble Martin lists it in *The Concise British Flora*, and it may well be distributed in Britain as a wild plant, although I don't think I have ever come across it or could identify it without a book in my hand.

Valerian, another "herb" mentioned, is a great nuisance here because its roots break down the mortar in the walls. We have no fewer than three colours, a strong red, a pink and a white. It is said to be a nerve tonic if a decoction is made of the roots, and the updated notes to the original Culpeper say it was used in the Middle Ages as a spice, and also to scent linen, although the smell of the plant is "very distasteful to some people".

MY COUNTRY GARDEN

I WAS up in the wood inspecting the defences which I had constructed to keep vandals out, when I spotted a seedling gooseberry. It was just budding and it was growing from a crevice below the limestone wall. My mind flicked through a whole series of images of fruit bushes in the wilderness. I used to know of a very fine bullace tree, and always intended to go back to it and pick the marble-sized "wild plums" to make wine from them, but birds got the fruit. My grand-mother, I remember, had her "secret" crab-apple tree in an unkempt hedge and went to it every year for crabs, which she blended with rowans to make jelly. She was a great harvester of wild fruits. If she didn't go to gather "rasps" herself, she made sure her daughters picked the "hindberries".

The luscious red or yellow raspberry from our gardens is there to prove what man can do to improve strains, but the wild gooseberry hardly ever bears fruit. It is invariably a degenerated bush. The bullace, which I have encountered only here in Wales, puzzles me. Is it really a degenerating plum, or is it a true native like the wild, uncultivated crab-apple? There are, of course, highly decorative, cultivated crab-apples. I remember seeing one growing wild with beautiful red-gold apples on it. The apples were small and hard and proved particularly sour when I sampled one. This "wild" crab-apple had obviously seeded in a hawthorn hedge a long way from any private garden in which such an ornamental tree could have been growing.

ENCOUNTERS with straying livestock are one of the penalties of living in a part of the world where fences are never very sound. This morning the bleating of a sheep alerted me to the danger of an invasion such as we had last summer, when a whole flock came down the lane to crop the few plants my wife had bedded outside. I hastened to forestall the invasion before it gained momentum and, while clattering down the steps waving a yard brush, used the shepherd's trick to get sheep on the run by whistling up an imaginary dog if the real one is unavailable.

To my dismay the sheep stopped in its tracks and turned about. Instead of running away and ignoring the brandished brush, the creature came running towards me. My neighbour evidently whistles his flock to the feeding troughs in winter. The misguided animal came on at a trot, but at the last minute dodged past me and went rushing down the lane. Now if I didn't proceed with caution I would be seen to be driving a sheep away from its pasture. Someone coming upon me might even take me for a sheep rustler, for sheep rustlers are in business in Wales as they haven't been since the days when it was found necessary to hang them.

The anticipated exodus didn't materialise. I studied the perimeter defences of the grazing. They seemed as intact as they had ever been, and I couldn't imagine how that sheep had got into the lane in the first place, unless it came over the stone stile. I am keeping a low profile at the moment, hoping the sheep has a strong homing instinct.

MY COUNTRY GARDEN

A QUEEN wasp, probably forced to leave her bank nest because of the most recent downpour, appeared at the window behind which I am at the moment sitting. In the corner of the sash a spider had put up a well-braced web into which the queen wasp blundered. The shaking of the "guy ropes" alerted the spider, a sizeable creature, who emerged from the timber of the windowframe.

For seconds the spider seemed to contemplate the outsized wasp and then retreated back into its lair. The queen wasp fought the entanglement and struggled to escape. Her wings remained free and I saw that she was actually biting at the web.

The spider ran out again but immediately lost its nerve and dashed back. The wasp didn't seem to notice that the spider was out and about, but her abdomen flexed as though she was making sure her sting was in order if needed.

All at once she broke free, falling an inch or two before her wings came into play and she could fly off. The spider appeared and hurried out to the hole the wasp had made. I expected to see a quick repair being done, but either the spider was too lazy to renovate the broken web or decided it was good enough to hold its normal kind of prey. The large queen wasp would have been a dangerous handful even had the web held.

AS one gets older, what was once significant becomes less so, and what was insignificant often becomes significant. Once I might have been in too much of a hurry to stop and look at what appeared to be a brown chipwood on the doorstep, but yesterday with a glass of my home-made beer in my hand, I regarded this object and wondered what it was until it moved.

Wedge-shaped because its wings were folded tent-wise over its body, it looked for all the world like a piece of polished oak, a chipping flown there when I had been splitting logs. On closer examination my lovely fragment of oak seemed to have two sets of wings, one over its back, and a pair forward that were, in fact, feathered antennae. The moth was a thorn, and perhaps not a very rare species, but I had to look it up to discover what it was. Looking up the moth brought me back to the wonderful system of naming that the entomologists hit upon for all the species they discovered. The thorn may bear some resemblance to a thorn or be named because it is found on thorny trees. But what about the wainscots, the burnished brass, the beautiful arches, the stranger and the lunar marbled brown, not to mention the rosy wave or the slender Scotch burnet?

Browsing through my reference books, I also discover that a host of what I would have called flies or wasps are clear-winged moths of the *sessiidae* family. One is, in fact, the hornet moth mainly encountered here in early summer, when it emerges from a chrysalis hosted by the poplar tree.

MY COUNTRY GARDEN

ONE of the delights of my childhood was the pursuit of butterflies across our meadows and along the hedges. I thought about my pursuit of the meadow brown and sometimes the Scotch argus yesterday when all at once a bright yellow butterfly came flitting across the lawn. For a moment I couldn't think what it could be. I dropped what I was doing and began to plod to the far corner of the lawn, crossing turf as soggy as a wet sponge and fearing that the butterfly, as butterflies always did when I was a child, would rise and sail away as I got up to it, but this didn't happen. I stood still at last close to the place where I had seen it settle and I discovered it, wings folded, lying on its side and imitating a yellow leaf.

It was a most perfect specimen of a brimstone, a butterfly I hadn't seen since leaving the south of England more than 40 years ago. The brimstone appearing in spring is invariably one not long emerged from hibernation, and is conspicuous on account of its bright sulphur colour. In the ordinary way the brimstone breeds up and becomes a common sight in June in localities where there is buckthorn, the host for its caterpillar. This information is from a book, I have to confess. Brimstones, according to the map, aren't found in the British Isles outside England and Wales. In southwest Scotland the Scotch argus used to be seen on the fringes of the moorland in mid-August. Although I knew it well and thought it the most lovely butterfly of all, I had gone from the locality before I was able to put a name to it.

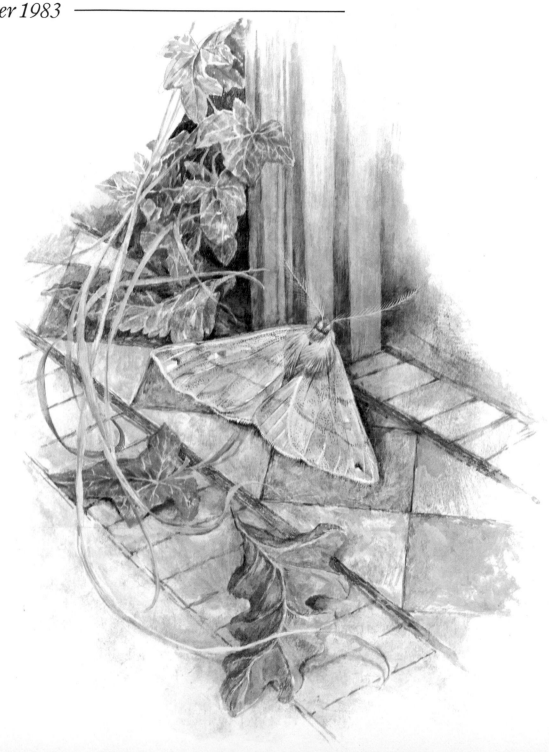

October 1983

WE were having a barbecue. It was a warm evening, and the chilled wine caused condensation on the glass. God seemed to be in his sunset heaven until I looked across the paddock and saw, lumbering towards us and sniffing the air like one of the old-time Bisto Kids, a lean and hungry brood sow. Her ears flapped. She looked a little short-sighted, and she had no fewer than ten grunting pink piglets at her heels. It could be a mirage, I told myself, or perhaps the wine was a little more potent than I had thought? A mirage fades, and pink elephants are what a wine biber is more likely to see.

Springing to my feet, I rushed to the gate in the paddock fence. The sow swung round and headed towards me. She evidently thought that I had a bucket of mash hidden about me somewhere. The piglets turned like cavalry in a flanking movement and joined their mother, but I had a stick and turned the charge, giving the sow a whack to encourage her to depart. The herd, for it had taken on herd proportions in my slightly befuddled state, careered downhill to the far corner of the second paddock. Knowing how pig-headed pigs can be, I had to follow to make sure they left the way they had come in. My anxiety to see them off started a Gadarene rush, and instead of turning uphill, to their devastated, turfless pasture, they went out on to the lane and on downhill, out of sight.

Conscience wouldn't allow me to leave things like this, for the lane is trafficked of a Saturday evening by all kinds of candidates for the breathalyser hurrying from one pub to another. I had hardly reached our lower gateway when I heard a car applying its brakes and a screech of tyres that alarmed me even more. I waited for the sound of the crash. I expected to see dead pigs flying through the air and landing on my side of the hedge, but then came the grunts and squeals of piglets punctuated by the bleeping of a car horn. The driver of the car brought the lot of them back and herded them, on his front bumper, into the entry and up to their field. He turned out to be the modern equivalent of the swineherd. Pigs, he told me, go where the mood takes them.

Not long ago the Post Office, ignoring the fact that we had printed stationery, informed me that the address is not Hog Lane or Hog Lane Hill. I think they should reconsider in the light of the foregoing. We cleared up the barbecue and drank the remainder of the wine, ignoring moths and midges. This was the end of a not exactly perfect day, for it had begun with two white-faced Herefords appearing on the lawn shortly after first light. Even with that stampede of swine, it wasn't over and done with: with no regard for the Sabbath, the sow came back in the morning, bringing reinforcements of ten extra bouncing, grunting piglets recruited from her sister's litter. After I had driven them all back three times, I went down and stapled a printed notice on to my absent neighbour's barn. It said, next time I shall barbecue two of your piglets, something I shall enjoy even if you may not!

MY COUNTRY GARDEN

WHEN my neighbour's two white-faced bullocks are full-grown, if they are spared that long, they will make passable stand-ins for the beef suet oxen that once pulled an advertising wagon on a tour of Britain. I can't say I ever got much response from bovine creatures, except for the time I was chased by an ill-tempered Galloway bull. The Herefords have continued to break through the fence at the far corner of our ground despite my efforts to keep them out. Now I have to go off and buy yet another spool of barbed wire to improve defences. For a while it was the sow and her litter. The

Herefords are something different. If they would only stay in the far corner I might manage to put up with their trespass, but alas, like the old sow, they have a hankering for pastures new. They plod steadily on after they have jumped a barrier of fallen trees and some of my best crochet work with wire and angle iron. Their curiosity brings them to the lawn. If they can kick up their heels and gallop about for a while they are satisfied and settle down to browsing on rambler roses.

I advance on the Herefords and they take all four feet off the ground, switch their tails and bounce off back into the wilderness. My neighbour now sends his men after them, but they make a poor job of it and go round and round in circles after the bullocks. I have to take a hand with the one remaining hayfork without a broken shaft. I broke two forkshafts in the pursuit of the sow without getting within striking distance of her. I have no chance of catching up with the Herefords. They go rushing out like bulls into a sunlit bullring and then tear on across their own sun-drenched field.

The trouble is they like the shade of our scrubland and they have the curiosity of cats. "I will have the beggars put down!" my neighbour promises me, but he never does. This, I am afraid, is what living in the country is about and having spent much of my childhood helping to get sheep from someone else's fields, bullocks from their back hills and wayward bulls from all the points of the compass, I shouldn't be too put out. I just get a little weary of it at times and wish I had a humane killer.

MY COUNTRY GARDEN

October 1983

THE season of mellow fruitfulness is, I suppose, the ripening of apples, pears and hedge fruits like bramble, elderberry, bullace and sloe. Here the fruitfulness is limited. The very old apple trees that grow on either side of the drive, having been over-productive in last season's glut, have hibernated. Only one or two have had a crop. Because the summer has been so dry, apples, scarred and scabbed because they weren't sprayed, have fallen every day. The windfall needed no wind, nor even a breeze. They would drop on the stillest of hot afternoons.

And if I go to pick blackberries to flavour a few windfalls gathered before wasps or the wheels of the milk truck get them, the berries are not as big as in the past and a lot of them are being ruined by blackbirds. It is a business of swings and roundabouts, good seasons and not so good seasons. I look for mushrooms and find puffballs which I like, although nothing beats a large, juicy horse mushroom and the ketchup-like gravy in which it swims when it is slid on to the plate from the pan.

I am not usually one to count my chickens before they are hatched, but I thought to harvest a bountiful crop of hazelnuts. The trees were laden with them until the squirrels got to work, chopping the nuts off the branch and leaving them nibbled on the ground. Perhaps the squirrels themselves didn't get the feast they expected. The nuts were big but hollow. I think this had something to do with drought following a wet spring. So we have no problem in storing apples or nuts.

November 1983

IT always seems to me that if we aren't competitors we are doomed to perish. Charity is one of the great human virtues, but if it thrives it does so because we have conscience. I compete, in my insignificance, with creatures that will take what I would have. The early bird doesn't just take the worm. He would take the vegetables from my garden. I escape this penalty for late rising because I don't grow vegetables, but the blackbird harvested the blackberries I wanted for wine-making. Pigeons came fluttering into the drooping branches of the elderberry bushes to gorge themselves on fruit. The fruits were here before I came, and birds have no conception of what ownership means. The mushrooms in the wet grass are only mine if I can get to them before the slugs. I suspect that even the squirrel has a taste for mushrooms, because the other morning, when I decided to leave a few half-grown ones to grow bigger, I returned to the spot to find that all that remained were the stalks. The mushrooms had been eaten by something with more dentures than a slug.

Through the day blackbirds peck at the apples and wasps sustain themselves and get drunk on the ferment as the bruised fruit rots. It is necessary to be out soon after the wind has dropped to pick windfalls. The few apples high on the old trees aren't plentiful enough to justify the labour involved in moving ladders around and getting them down. I might come to earth faster than I ascended into those trees with old branches as fragile as last year's crow's nest. I am reconciled to my tithe. There will be enough for all.

MY COUNTRY GARDEN

CURIOSITY may have killed many cats, or the saying would be meaningless, I suppose, but cats are not the only creatures who suffer from uncontrollable curiosity. Heifers and bullocks must be high on the list. If they are ignored, cattle will almost invariably come to poke their noses into what man is doing.

The white-faced Hereford that had come in under two strands of barbed wire to explore our lower paddock couldn't have thought that she was trespassing, although I knew nothing about it until she was there at my elbow. I was so startled that I must have been on the verge of cardiac arrest. The Hereford jumped back, too, at full length, bouncing on stiff legs as she did so. I waved my arm to frighten her away, but in a minute she was back at my elbow. I noticed the steam from her nostrils even before I heard the intestinal rumbling. I waved more threateningly and she made another stiff-legged bounce and stood like a statue. So I made a dive towards her, waving the wire I had been trying to fix to the fence to secure the gate, and she galloped down the paddock. I knew she would be back, and the third time I had to rout her altogether. She went in panic over the wire at the far corner and down on to the lane.

I wondered if it could be considered my responsibility to go after and put her back where she belonged, but decided it wasn't. I could have been running about all day securing animals that weren't mine and have ended up with motorists shaking their fists at me.

AS anyone who has had close encounters with pigs will know, nothing, except a four or multi-furrow plough, ploughs land faster than a rooting sow. There might be a future in it if someone could train a pig to plough in a straight line, but alas, they tend to root in circles. The phantom sow that came last summer returned in the early hours of this morning, although at first what I thought we had was a high-speed mole throwing up hills.

I looked down the drive from an upstairs window and could hardly believe my eyes. The sow, or sows, had gone by this time, but when I had hauled on my boots and hurried down to investigate I found the unmistakable signature of that wayward breed. My hard labour clearing brambles, and mowing the orchard grass a dozen times last summer, had been sabotaged, and, given half a chance, the saboteurs would come back. I typed a note for my neighbour, summoning him to the scene as soon as possible and demanding that he put the things right, and delivered the message to his man at the piggery. The orchard, it seemed to me, could even be planted with potatoes so long as the pigs didn't come back to eat them before they sprouted.

My neighbour, who had come in at daybreak to remove his pigs, was back here by mid-morning replacing the turf and making the place tidy. What more could he do?

MY COUNTRY GARDEN

THE trouble with apple trees, it seems to me, is that, like man, they get past their prime. Even though they may become crabbed and old there is something beautiful about them. Like old oaks they become venerable. A young tree may be smooth-barked and virile, and bear a reasonable crop even in a poor season, but the old tree has character. It survives in spite of its canker and its host of parasites, and it stands where some long-dead gardener lovingly set it in the earth and tended it in the days of its infant nurture.

This is a sentimental viewpoint, but then I have always inherited old trees, and have never judged them by the harvest they gave me. An old tree is like an old house, and who would live in the sculpture of incurved concrete perpetrated by the modern architect if he could live in a Victorian or Elizabethan house (not that I live in such a house myself)!

In our very first garden in North Wales there was a very old apple tree that grew on the steeply sloping ground higher than the level of our bedroom windows. It didn't bear much fruit until I accidentally shot it when I scared some jackdaws from the peas one summer's afternoon. The shot cut the bark of the tree, and after that we had apples as never before. The old people said I had done a better job than if I had ringed or root-pruned.

When we moved to the cottage, I inherited perhaps 60 very old trees. Some of them were impossible to identify. The varieties had gone out of fashion 50 years before, but still, once in a blue moon, bore delicious dessert apples and superb cookers. I didn't shoot them, although I should perhaps have cut them down to prevent disease spreading to the little orchard I planted on the far side of the cottage.

Those old apples went right back to the garden of Eden, an expert gardener once laughingly remarked, but even the trees I put in tended to go out of fashion in the two and a half decades that followed. When we moved here I inherited more old trees. The ones at the cottage were all wire-trained, espaliers, fan-trained, and cordons. But here they are the everyday orchard tree, long left unpruned and with intertwined branches that have knitted their twigs into a fabric that would call for major surgery to put things right. What really delighted me in our first spring was the blossom, for although we had no apple crop to speak of, we had a wonderful display of pink-tinged and white blossom. The old trees were a sight to behold, and shortly now, with any luck, that vision will be ours again.

MY COUNTRY GARDEN

THE problem of keeping a tract of land reasonably wild and natural, so that birds and animals thrive in cover, is how to cope with the seeding of weeds no one wants. It may delight the naturalist to see ragwort, willow bay herb and Scotch thistles in flower on an uncared for pasture or tract of scrubland, but people beyond the boundary often abhor the weeds. They may even make a complaint and bring the law to bear on the man who harbours them.

What should I do about it? Willow bay herb can be discouraged by repeated cutting back, and perhaps it finally gives up. Nettles need more drastic treatment. When I have both under control, a mower may cut creeping brambles at ground level until they, too, give up, but the small voice of conscience asks if such order is really what I want. I must prove to myself that I am not just lazy. Order there must be, and then some kind of controlled naturalisation: corners in which willow bay herb will grow like hollyhock, perhaps a mound clothed with lovely green nettle like aubrietia on a rockery, and blackberry bushes left to cover young pheasants or provide something for the muntjac to browse upon.

All of this, but order first. I suppose I am inhibited by a recollection of my elders saying that weeds advertised laziness, bad husbandry and the indolence of people "God had no time for", although I never heard of Adam doing much more in the garden than eating an apple which he didn't pick for himself.

LAST spring, when the first paddock was newly fenced and my neighbour's ponies were about to be brought in, fearing for the survival of the cowslips I found growing there, I hurried over with a spade and a wheelbarrow and dug the whole lot up so that I could replant them on the other side of the lawn. It was a good thing that I did so, even if what I did might, in the eyes of the law and the conservationist, have seemed an offence. The ponies proved themselves omnivorous and devoured every stalk and stem of greenery on the ground before they munched on the bark of trees, creating devastation that would have delighted a conquering warlord.

Cowslips used to grow on the clifftop at the cottage and we were careful not to pick them or tell anyone they were there. Much earlier, cowslips had once been abundant on rough land on the sea cliffs further along the coast. Their abundance advertised itself and soon all the roots were taken and the fields left bare. Here the transplanted cowslips are growing naturally in rough grass by the side of what was once an airing green, and I am delighted.

When the sows got in not long ago, they rooted up the turf on one side of the drive, and hundreds of primroses were destroyed. It saddened me for I had been careful to set the rough grass-cutter so that the plants escaped. One can't really plan for things like cowslips and primroses, wild violets or bluebells. Like honeysuckle in the hedge, they are a natural inheritance and all the more beautiful growing where and when they appear.

MY COUNTRY GARDEN

THE sights and scents of summer, in contrast to the way the grass grows after the previous mowing and an overnight downpour, are the delight of the season, whether it rains or shines. What is more intoxicating than the scent of May blossom, honeysuckle and meadowsweet? Like too much wine or cool bitter on a hot summer's day, these olfactory pleasures can become intoxicating, and overpowering, and one must move away from the rain-stimulated hawthorn and wild woodbine to appreciate them again.

Meadowsweet fills me with nostalgia. It was part of the scent of the wilderness, the peat moss with its banks of bilberry and fringes of fern I knew so well as a boy. I never breathe that scent without walking with my aunts down to the country schoolhouse to a "preaching". They were deeply religious and gave all their attention to the minister, while I could never stop my mind from wandering back to the mint-scented ditch that fed the burn along which meadowsweet and yellow flags grew.

One of the advantages of getting on in years is to be able to recall a richer world of experience. At this moment we look out on the far paddock where the willow bay herb is slowly coming on, after its flailing last summer, and struggling to take over from that other common wilderness plant that has the lovely name of sweet cicely. This plant, moving in a gentle breeze, looks like the background of some classic impressionist painting, but beyond our boundary is a long field of barley, and when the wind is on it, it is as though waves were being urged towards the shoreline of the hedge. This, too, is nostalgic for me, since we grew barley for the distillery.

Is it not a marvellous thing that, when we have lost the cherry blossom, the apple and the pear bloom, and then the green thorn and the mountain ash and the broom, we still have the gorse? Kissing is not in season when the gorse is not in bloom, they say, because somewhere all the year round, it is possible to find just a little bit of gorse bloom. It may be an everlasting nuisance to the farmer, but, in high summer in some places, it is a display of dark green and gold, richer than the finest butter a dairymaid ever churned.

November 1984

THIS must surely have been the year of the fungus, for I have never seen so many kinds, or any one species, in such abundance. Almost every day I have gone back to my reference books to check on something I haven't seen before, but even the better of the two books isn't quite good enough to tell me what I can eat and what I should avoid. I wonder what they mean when they advise caution, for instance. Should I sample just a little of the thing and wait and see whether I hallucinate or not? No book on fungi ever comes up to expectation when one is seeking culinary advice. Edible fungi that are entirely safe one might count on the fingers of both hands. Really poisonous sorts aren't particularly numerous, but the problem lies in the fact that certain things are edible at an early stage in their growth and emetic when they are full-grown, while others shouldn't be stewed. What we need is a taster. A feast grew on the lawn some weeks ago if I only had had the courage to put some of the picking in a stewpan. Some looked like liver. One or two had a turquoise colour and were partially luminous. Without looking at the book, one knew that they would have a less than pleasant taste and might be as lethal as the fly agaric or the death cap.

The majority of these growths followed the appearance of the field and the horse mushroom. We had a blusher or two, and more puffballs than last year. I walked about day after day, picking the new arrivals and smelling them, although smell isn't a reliable guide, and the theory of inedible fungus turning a silver spoon black is a nega-tive thing. It comes down to safety first – all snakes are adders and all bulls are enraged by the sight of a red cloth. Hallucinations are frightening because the subject doesn't know if he will ever come back to normal. I suppose some people are prepared for the "trip" and illusion is more satisfactory than reality. There was either a feast or the makings of an orgy that grew on the lawn, but later on the sun dried the grass enough to let me run the mower over it, and the whole lot were chopped up: those fairy rings sprinkled with toadstools and all those clusters of mahogany-coloured fungi larger than the palm of my hand.

MY COUNTRY GARDEN

November 1984

GOOSEBERRIES are out of fashion, I read somewhere the other day. I doubt that this is true. Anyone who has ever tasted a gooseberry pie or eaten gooseberry jam will see that the bush is never neglected. When I was a boy we used to have two kinds of gooseberry jam, red and green, and the old kitchen garden had several dessert gooseberries that bore enormous crops, which I always did my best to demolish, even when they had the same laxative effect as the black treacle kept to supplement the diet of our cattle.

It was about time someone reminded me of the luscious gooseberries that grew in our first garden in North Wales. They were a hairless variety, bigger than damsons and twice as sweet. Looking at the garden catalogue, I thought to replace them, even if I had never discovered the name of the variety, and sent off for a couple of bushes, forgetting about the dozen other urgent chores to be performed before I could think of planting fruit bushes. No matter, the thing was done, and shortly the postman hammered on the front door to deliver the package. Common sense told me they must be planted as soon as possible or I would have to wait another year, watching the dried-out roots of my gooseberries die.

I read up on planting the things, barrowed some special compost, manure and peat, down to the far end, and set about double-digging as recommended in the book. It took longer than I thought, and when I had done and pruned my bushes, also according to the book, they looked like nothing; but who can tell? We have a long way to go to another midsummer and gooseberry pies.

It isn't so much the remembered taste of gooseberries sweeter than wine, but nostalgia for a time when I would crouch down, hidden from my elders, and eat the ripe fruit of the kitchen garden until I could take no dinner.

November 1985

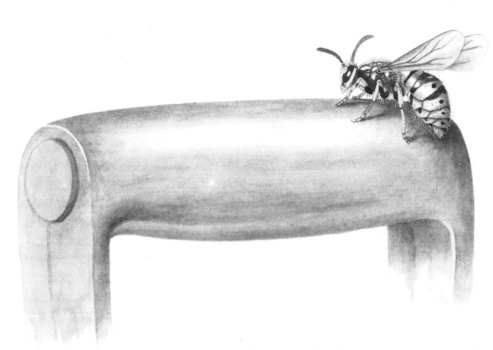

ators, or the occasional visitor like Topsy who steals in behind me and gets very excited if a butterfly flits across the building. She has a taste for butterflies that harks back to her days at the cottage when she pursued them in the open and devoured them on the few occasions when she managed to claw one out of the air.

I was in the shed the other day when I disturbed a "hibernator", a long-bodied queen wasp, for wasps like to tuck themselves away in as warm a place as they can find, emerging in the spring to start the business all over again as they construct nests in banks or hang their papier maché creations under eaves. The Chinese lantern sort of nest is made by a type of wasp who begins with a miniature work of art the size of a walnut and goes on, when the pickings are good, to construct something as big or even bigger than a man's head. I never quite know what I should do about wasps. They aren't aggressive unless disturbed, which is like most human beings. They do a great deal to keep down the insect parasites we don't want; altogether they play an important part in the ecological system.

I let the queen wasp find a new place in the overlapping timber and hoped she would be responsible in due course for keeping down mosquitoes and other flying, biting pests that rise from the long grass in summer. I received my last wasp sting when I was picking up windfalls and put my hand on a wasp drunk on apple juice. If I had looked carefully it wouldn't have happened.

ALTHOUGH it is showing its age and becoming a little the worse for wear in places, what was once an old wooden stable at the far corner of the garden is really a quite snug haven for a number of creatures to come in out of the cold. Mice have their quarters under the timber stacked along one wall. Birds can squeeze in through a gap in the weatherboarding. Wrens once nested near the window. The fat-tailed dormice come and go and probably hibernate where the timber is heavy and unlikely to be moved.

Butterflies try to find quarters until spring, but of course they may have to contend with insect pred-

MY COUNTRY GARDEN

WHEN I was a boy my father, who was an engineer, bought me a Meccano set that would today be a collector's item, I suppose. It was one of those early-day, unpainted kits of perforated metal strips and plates, sprocket wheels, crank handles and nuts and bolts. The whole thing made up an outfit that might, according to its number, enable a boy to construct a wheelbarrow or even Sydney Bridge, if the bridge was there, as I suppose it was, something like 60 years ago.

All this comes to mind, along with the frustration I had fiddling with nuts and bolts and unmanageable stays and angle brackets, because I have been working with an assembly kit designed to leave me the proud possessor of a greenhouse. I must say, moments of frustration and self-inspired fury excepted, I have enjoyed myself. Some people might say I am enjoying a second boyhood if not my second childhood. The plan was to have some help in assembling the final structure after I had Meccano-ed the components, the sides and the gables, doors and ventilators, and the rest. In the end, having already laid the foundation, square and level, I went on to do the whole thing myself. There wasn't a foreman in sight to tell me it was time for a teabreak, or time me with a stopwatch. Respecting my employer, I told him I would do my best for him if he did his best for me and got on with the thing.

A robin was my overseer two days running. Robins are interested in human activity, I am sure of that. We have one who looks into the sitting room from a vantage point on the corner of the loggia roof, and it was this bird that came and sat on the back gate to watch me assembling the glazing bars and the bracing struts of the greenhouse framework. I occasionally straightened my aching back, or rose from my knees, to clear the concrete of bits of gravel that made the kneeling unbearable, and spoke to the robin. He cocked his head and seemed to know what pain was in it, but I was amazed, two days later, to find him there at the far end of the old fruit garden, watching final assembly. I hadn't a crumb to offer him.

I had treated the ground earlier so that the earth within the enclosure hadn't a worm or insect in it, but the bird wasn't there to beg. He had come out of curiosity to see what I was up to now. He departed after a little while to find food in the bushes, but he came again while I was glazing the roof and left his card on the glass. Perhaps in another life he had been a keen gardener? I could have done with his advice whether he had been a gardener or a construction engineer, though he may simply have been a Meccano-owning schoolboy.

SKETCHES
OF
BIRDLIFE

There are several ways of encouraging birds to come to your doorstep. The most important one is to provide the food they like best, such as seed, peanuts and fat, though some birds happily settle for bread. At the birdtables, the traffic includes tits, greenfinches, blackbirds, starlings, nuthatches, and the great spotted woodpecker, who intimidates the smaller birds. The starlings are bullies; the magpie is a sneak thief. I have recorded 22 species at the birdtables in a single day in winter.

Two tawny owls who live in the dead oak on the rockery perched regularly on the birch stump last summer. Of the barn owl there is no sign. I have a feeling they have gone from this part of the world altogether, and this saddens me. Barns have gone and the habitat of the handsome barn owl with them. I sigh when I think that they used to nest in the farm chimney when I was a child. Sent to bed early, I would lie awake listening to the excited barn owl chicks as their parents came on to the chimney stack and dropped them the mice they had caught. There were corncrakes in the long grass in those days, and I thought in my innocence that barn owls and corncrakes would be with us forever.

December 1971

IT was, I think, a great summer for the waterhen, despite the lack of rain, for I never saw so many on the stream that adjoins the shoot. Waterhens, or moorhens as some people prefer to call them, thrive in ponds and drains adjoining boggy land. They explore far and wide from these wet areas, providing the ground is not too well drained and dry. They are great runners, but they can be quite unobtrusive as they weave their way in and out of scrub trees and hedges adjoining the marsh. On occasions, like the partridge, they will perch in the bush and fly from it, going low across the field and trailing their legs for the touchdown, close to the cover of rushes or bank weeds.

Yesterday, walking up the stream, which winds through the farms where cattle and sheep are now wandering freely across the stubbles, I counted waterhens until I had to give up. They were everywhere, swimming on the open water, slipping through under the overhanging bushes and brambles, burying themselves in the cress and green weed covering shingle banks. They feed on a great variety of things, from grain and weed to molluscs and worms. The keeper doesn't welcome them because they will take food he puts down for his birds, or the mallard coming in to his ponds. He blames them for taking gamebird eggs and I suppose must have proof of this, although a waterhen seems an unlikely egg thief to me.

Long ago, when I was a boy, I loved to go in search of the waterhen's nest. It was one of the idle things a boy, without company of his own age, could do on a bright sunny day. The waterhen's nest could be anywhere, lodged in the trailing branch of a thorn, inches from the surface of the water, or away out on a quagmire of heaving black peat, woven into the support of a stunted round rush clump. One got wet exploring for the waterhen's nest, but boots and stockings were removed, the stockings pushed into the boots, and these hung around one's neck by tying the laces together. In a short time the woollen stockings would be replaced by stockings of black mud, but the mud would wash off, and it was always soft and cool to the touch.

I never looked at a clutch of eggs on one of those rush rafts fashioned by the elusive waterhen without holding my breath at the beauty of the thing. When the eggs hatch it is only a short time before the blacker-than-black waterhen chicks are paddling away. Only occasionally did I catch one and hold it in the palm of my hand before releasing it again. Until yesterday I hadn't seen quite so many waterhens as I had known in my youth. I had, in fact, come to think that pollution was having some effect upon their breeding, and that they might be on the decline.

February 1972

THE hooded crow, or hoodie, as it is commonly called in Scotland where the grey-mantled bird is seen as often as, and indeed sometimes more often, than the ordinary carrion crow, comes along our coast once in a while as a migrant. It has been here often enough to have Welsh names, and those names prove that the old Welsh bird-watchers could give an apt description. They called it *bran glan y mor* – the sea-shore crow, *bran yr Iwerddon* – the Irish crow or *bran y lludw*, the ashy crow. An old book tells me that one was trapped on the shore of a mountain lake near Betws y Coed in 1880, but the hoodie was more often on the seaboard plains, and rarely got up to the grouse moors; rarely also did it remain to breed. Once in a while there were reports of hybrids for, of course, the hooded bird is a sub-species of the genus.

It is hard to say why we are without hooded crows in Wales. It is a common crow in Ireland. It is resident in the Isle of Man, I believe, and feeding on the same things as its all-black relative, the carrion crow, of which we have more than our share. There is no reason why it shouldn't live with us. Perhaps it once did, or it may be that, like the winter stoat of the north, there is something

about the landscape in the places where it is found that induces the breeding of the grey bird, and to a slight degree, discourages the all-black one.

The sea-shore crow is a good name for the hooded crow because its migration tends to be coastal. Even in the north, where it breeds, it shows a decided preference for off-shore islands. There is a forbidding greyness about the hoodie, when one sees him in his native place. He looks as though he scavenged in the Tundra. His background is desolation, snow blots and a biting wind, so far as I am concerned, but then I saw him most often in my boyhood, and associate him with the grim north, chapped hands, frozen furrows and a seemingly endless winter.

December 1972

BIRDS intrude very little into our world. The gulls bother us occasionally, but as a general rule we are the intruders and we cause the disturbance if there is any. I thought about this yesterday when I suddenly became aware of the jackdaws up in the tops of the pine trees. A fight was going on. Only two birds were involved, as is almost always the case.

The two birds in this case had come tumbling down out of the higher branches. The gallery was excited and looked down at the fighting pair as they whirled on down to the long grass beneath the trees. Some of the spectators moved their positions to get a better view. The clamour couldn't be ignored and it was drawing more and more birds from round about. When the birds broke off and flew back aloft the crowd didn't disperse. They knew it wasn't over. One or two cawed angrily as though urging the contestants to get on with it.

I walked up the path. The birds ignored me. They were deeply involved in this thing and I didn't exist. I was convinced of this when the two fighters set to again and came down almost at my feet. They were in a frenzy. The gallery's stare made me look up. One or two of them saw me and cawed. The warning was there. The fighting birds must have heard it quite clearly, for they flew up in sudden fright. The jackdaws flapped on along the top of the trees and I could hear sounds of a renewal of the fight. Some of the spectators milled around in the air above the trees and then there was silence. One by one the crowd dispersed.

MY wife was telling me about a friend of hers who would regularly go out and "converse" with owls that perched in the trees close to her house, establishing a kind of association with them as one might with a blackbird or sparrow coming to the back door. I have found that the tawny owls that haunt our wood and frequent the trees above the cottage at certain times show a marked curiosity about what goes on in the court. They respond to my making owl-like noises through my cupped hands and fly closer in an effort to discover what sort of creature is trying to be an owl. They stare into the strong beam of my handlight, but not for long, and flit away into more shadowed places, yet they will keep up an almost endless conversation. Their responses, I am sure, bring other owls closer. I often have a feeling that small though a bird's brain may be, they study us almost as much as we study them and with about as much useful purpose. Perhaps even more, since their survival often seems to depend on knowing just how dangerous and untrustworthy we can be.

July 1973

THE sparrowhawk swims in the air like a powerful fish in the stream, going at top speed, but twisting and turning and avoiding obstacles with the skill of a racing driver. Watching one yesterday, I found my heartbeat quickening at the speed and dash of the streamlined bird. How many hundreds of times a minute must its eyes focus and refocus to enable it to see things in its way, and how swift must its reaction be to let it take avoiding action. There are few birds that can do this kind of thing. The sparrowhawk and the goshawk were designed for speed and what the aircraft designer calls manoeuvrability. The truth is that had they not developed in this way they would have ceased to be hawks and would have become mainly carrion eaters.

When I had a sparrowhawk I made a study of their hunting. They seemed to me to be far short of vicious in the fact that they do not chase their quarry until they are hungry. Unlike the stoat or the fox, they don't kill for killing's sake and will sit quietly digesting the contents of a crop until the source of energy is exhausted. They now show a more active interest in the world around them. They become more vigilant and restless and finally take off on patrol, skirting flocks of birds, coming up on them in a peculiarly indirect way until, all at once, a sort of alarm rings. The quarry becomes nervous and excited. The hawk is on edge. The chase and the kill are triggered off. In a short time a small bird will be dead. Nothing in nature seems more perfectly arranged than the relationship between hunter and hunted in this particular case.

August 1973

THE stormcock doesn't sing so much in summer when it is nesting, but the mistle thrush's habit of perching high on a branch and singing in the face of a gale or downpour persists in the common thrush, which also warbles happily before rain. The lesser stormcocks were warbling this morning and I didn't need to go and look at the barometer to see if we were in for a heavy shower. Apart from the carrying of sound on moist air, which always makes us nod and look to see if there is any washing to be brought in from the line, the warbling of the thrushes is our most reliable warning of rain. I suppose there must be a negative thing to it too, for the chiffchaff which abounds here and sings from spring well on into summer falls silent when the sky begins to be overcast. The finches skulk in bushes, the wren, whose little song is most beautiful, scuttles into shelter like a mouse. The robin stands under a bush getting a little wet and bedraggled like a man taking cover on his way home.

We need rain, and the singing of the thrush is joyful perhaps because the bird senses that the moisture will bring worms and other creatures to the surface, and snails wandering from caverns beneath boulders. The seed-eating birds are less enthusiastic because seeds are washed into the grass and no longer drift where they can easily be picked up. It rains, and the grass and weeds seem to grow another foot in height, but if they do, the beetroots fatten, the lettuce take heart, and the winter broccoli already planted become a stronger shade of green and more healthy.

SKETCHES OF BIRDLIFE

NOT being a scientific person, I am unlikely to produce a monograph on any kind of bird, but if I embarked on such a thing the subject would almost certainly be the cormorant. I thought about this yesterday when I watched a line of them beating out over a leaden sea, flying only a few feet from the surface of the water. They flew round a headland where the wind could make a man's cheeks bleed, it is so fierce and cold, and went on eastwards to an estuary up the coast. They are the bird I always think closest to the reptile. They live a hard life and they are almost indestructible. They remain on the sea and fish it when all other divers have taken themselves off. They actually go down to keep warm, I think, when the air is freezing and splintered glass icicles are forming on trickles of water running over the sands.

The reptilian image persists when they are at roost, sitting in company and waiting for the turn of the tide. Now they might be lizards or some other sort of desert reptile, because their expression, if one watches through glasses, is blank, not contemplative, but as though they waited for time to pass. By comparison with other feathered predators, they are relentless. They have a fearful coldness about them. If a boy climbs to the ledges on which the colony nests he may take his life in his hands. They have the minute brain of a savage pike or a shark. One can believe that they came out of the water at the end of a phase of development. It was touch and go whether they were to be feathered or scaled.

The cormorant, along with the wild duck and the greylag goose, excited me when I was a small boy because it made daily flights across the countryside where my grandfather farmed, travelling from Wigtown Bay to Luce Bay in Galloway. It was known as a Mochrum skart, because, I suppose, its commonest flight line was across a place called Mochrum within the estate of Sir Herbert Maxwell of Monreith. The skarts never travelled in large numbers as did the geese, but in twos and threes. They flew high enough to be out of gunshot, but seemed to fly lower on moorland. The cormorants move to fish where the fish are. As the weather hardens, fishing in the open sea gets poorer. The upper reaches of estuaries are good places for small flounders. Tides and inland rainfall must affect the food supply. The inbuilt instinct of the birds tells them where to go, and when to move from the rocks of the shore to the creeks where they can dive and fish.

November 1974

SEEING a large and leisurely flight of Canada geese in echelon formation as they crossed the motorway one afternoon last week, I found myself wondering if anyone has an idea of how many of these North American geese we now have in Britain. I wonder, too, if anyone has studied them to see if these descendants of geese that followed a migratory course on the American flight line show any tendency to move in a north to south direction with the onset of colder weather.

Only incoming, early greylags and pinkfeet are comparatively tame, and they are generally young birds. The older migrants are reminded of their reception on our shores and estuaries as soon as they sight them again. The Canadas, however, being semi-tame and looked after on a great many private lakes and sanctuaries, are not harassed so much on their daily passage from one place to another. I have never shot at a Canada goose. There were only a few private "collections" of them when I was a boy, and none appeared over the Solway or more westerly parts of the country then. Now I wish I had never bothered any species of fowl, for all of them, from the diminutive teal to the big Canada which weighs considerably more than a greylag, are a wonderful spectacle.

A great company of Canadas is to be seen on one of the meres on the Shropshire border. A few weeks ago I was greatly taken by the sight of young, immature Canadas paddling in company, perhaps two or three hundred of them, all with their heads upraised to watch a flight of talkative older birds passing over in the opposite direction. In the traffic on the water, coots, waterhens and not a few mallards dodged in and out as they attempted to cross the path of the Canada goslings. It was all very amusing to watch, for as far as the geese were concerned the lesser fowl didn't exist. The adult birds were taking off into the wind, and I waited to see if any of the youngsters would do likewise, but they didn't. Instead a sort of guards counter-marching began. This was just as fascinating to watch, although the pattern soon vanished. The geese hadn't been trained by a drill sergeant, and the great company pressing on, milled until they were out of order and the mob they had become, turned and paddled in the opposite direction.

SKETCHES OF BIRDLIFE

A ROBIN is my shadow now. He haunts me when I am anywhere in the garden. I begin to wonder if he isn't Susy, our Cairn terrier, reincarnated, for he takes the same sort of interest in what I am doing and gets under my feet at times. I talk to him and he actually perches and sings to me, although I may be mistaken, failing to hear some other robin singing and encouraging my tame bird to respond. I have to be careful not to step on the little fellow. Yesterday while I was busy forking manure on to a newly-dug plot he actually came and perched on my back. He follows me into the pheasant pen and into the hut where I fill the can to feed the hens and where he has come to expect a crumb from the loaf I keep for the ducks. It is spring, and he has a companion close at hand, but his chosen mate is wary and keeps her distance. Perhaps she isn't a native but a continental bird. The European robin, as distinct from the British bird, is said to be quite shy and not given to perching on the spade or responding to overtures in the way our Christmas card little bird does. Two other birds have become very tame of late; they are a hedge sparrow that likes the henrun, and a blackbird that hovers about when I go out in the morning. A mouse-like wren flits in and out of the henhouse when I open up, but remains as wild as a field mouse and goes past my head like a bullet if I happen to enter the henhouse while she is stealing insects from the spiders' webs.

August 1976

THE gull is there first thing in the morning, standing on the slate paving beyond the kitchen window. He is generally there until it is time to go to roost, or sail aloft, whichever way he spends the night, and I have come to think of him as a fixture, a beggar with a chosen pitch, conditioned to the hand-out rather than with a natural bent for fending for himself. He does not plead. He just stands there and he knows that this pays off better than yelping or any of the other noises he might make.

I find a slice of bread and throw it out to him. He does not pick at it as a hen or even a crow might do, but bolts it down whole. I can see it, if it happens to be a hard slice, its outline, loaf-shaped, in his throat. He looks steadily at me as though to say "What about another?" I throw another, and he somehow lines it up in his craw alongside the first. If I threw him a whole loaf, slice by slice, I swear he would reassemble it. When I can find no bread I throw him not cake, but biscuits. He takes those the same way, but sometimes he reassembles them in packet form.

He could take an entire packet of wholemeal biscuits, I am sure of that, but after two or three I do a quick calorie calculation and cry enough. I have often stoked the greedy so-and-so with enough for a week. He is really posing for the camera. What I should do is to get the biscuit company to come down and do a commercial on him with a slogan – he could not get by without his daily wholemeal biscuits.

SKETCHES OF BIRDLIFE

ANTHROPOMORPHISM is a description scientific people just love to pin on "animal lovers", who desperately try to read things into animal behaviour that somehow put themselves and their pets on the same wavelength. In my own case I indulge in the thing with a touch of whimsy. Even as I am doing it I try to stand back and look at myself with amusement, which is very hard to do without luring out the psychiatrist with his own box of labels. This morning, catching a glimpse of our heavy-footed gull as it crash-landed on its way from the flat top of the dormer window to the sloping roof of the garage, I rushed out to have a word with it. I felt there was no time like the present for bringing good news to that rather lugubrious sea bird, who, like the young lady on the beach, has decided never to get her swimsuit wet.

The good news came in the mail from a gentleman with considerable interest in the business of making biscuits. My correspondent has an apparent compassion for hand-fed gulls who come to depend on human beings to a shameful extent. It was a short letter. I had committed it to memory. I recited the relevant part to the gull. It glissaded on its outsize feet, progressing downhill entirely against its will, for a gull's feet have no grip on wet and algaed asbestos. "You are in luck," I said. "A gentleman whose companies make the digestive biscuits we both love, and you consume at a ratio of between five and ten to my one, has most kindly offered to send you a packet or two. What do you think of that?"

Gulls, I must admit, have never said anything intelligible to me. I have heard them shriek with laughter, cry scornfully when the cat has just missed getting them as they flapped off the ground, and they have kept me awake at night with their private conversations, but never said a word I could guess at.

One might think, however, that a gull who has taken yards of bread from one's hand, and packet after packet of biscuits, would say something at the news that its appetite might be further gratified. The bird didn't utter a sound. It simply stayed there. I went indoors to look for a digestive biscuit, without success I am sorry to say. Time means nothing to animals. The gull must have thought the letter meant instant delivery. I popped my head out to suggest that it might say one word of thanks I could pass on, but it went on looking at me like a china ornament.

There's a thing, I thought. All over the town, down below, people are working towards the undoing of the herring gull. I get this one an "in" with a great commercial enterprise and it doesn't bat an eyelid. Serve it right, if, when the biscuits come, I eat them all myself.

January 1978

MY acquaintance with ravens has always been a remote one. I have looked into their nests at times. I have observed them flying over when I have been fishing. Since I have lived at the cottage I have had an equally remote contact with them, but a daily one because every morning they fly cronking over the roof and sometimes pass only 20 or 30 feet above our chimney pots. Now there has been a slight change in the behaviour of our ravens, who undoubtedly nest on cliff crags and patrol along our cliff for the enjoyment of the air currents and the thermals they encounter on hot days. The ravens have taken to perching in the pines for quite long periods, talking to one another as they sway on the very tips of the highest branches. They come in at different times in the day now where once they passed over mainly in the morning in the first hour or two. This may be due to some disturbance in the area in which they roost. Our old hens always scold when the ravens fly over. Indeed, they do this whatever species of bird, bigger than a thrush, crosses their line of vision. A cock pheasant taking flight annoys them. The magpie raises their blood pressure and the whole of the crow tribe is an abomination to them. Ravens perched keep the hen flock with one eye cocked in their direction. The ravens themselves never settle comfortably, but are content to bob up and down as the wind catches them or moves the branch upon which they are precariously balanced.

I have to conceal myself to observe them for, unlike the crows who know the strength of every move I make, the larger birds are uneasy at the very first glimpse of man either moving in their direction or standing watching them. When disturbed they will launch themselves into the air and, with a few powerful wingbeats, set themselves gliding out from the wood, ascending all the time by their ability to operate what the pilot calls the trailing edge or the aileron. This regular use of the pine wood intrigues me. I wonder if it is not a sign of the raven's world here contracting and the pressure of human encroachment on their lives building up. What will happen next if this is the case? Will the birds move off to a less-urbanised part of the world? They need a certain hunting territory. I am sure they also have a kind of living-space toleration which cannot be reduced.

Long ago, before poisonous sprays began to affect the peregrine, that wonderful bird began to leave most of the sea cliffs hereabouts, and it may be that our ravens are on the move in a similar way, for they never perched here before, except for a very occasional and fleeting moment. These things take a long time to work out, of course. Perhaps I shall only know the answer when it occurs to me that I no longer hear the ravens flying over, and never see one except when I go up into the hills to fish. This would be very sad.

SKETCHES OF BIRDLIFE

A READER writes to me from Italy about my remarks on the raven. "Your comments interested me because when river fishing in north-east Iceland, one frequently hears the raven's croak overhead. This is considered a good omen for the chances of landing a salmon from the pool one is at. It has never worked out that way with me. I am sure you know that all birds are protected in Iceland with the exception of the goose, which gobbles up grass that should make hay for winter feed, the only other predator being the red fox. In our area in September, one sees the ravens in the valley all collecting together which the locals call the raven's parliament. At this time they decide who will go to which farm to spend the winter months. It is a traditional rite among the local farmers to feed and house the ravens during the winter months. In return the ravens become airborne watch dogs and are an invaluable aid to the farm as look-outs. One calls to mind the ravens in the Tower of London, also those kept in Subiaco in Lazio Province. St Benedict is said to have been fed by them during a hard winter, and the story goes that the raven drank the poison that was meant for St Benedict."

I must say I had no idea the raven had such a place in folklore in so many different parts of the world. In my childhood it was regarded mainly as a rather ominous black bird, an outsize in crows that made people think of the undertaker. One particular raven I knew was the scourge of the children at the local country school, catching them as they crossed the small bridge over the burn, as they had to do on their way home, and pecking painfully at their bare legs.

When they stoned him in retaliation he would flap off cursing. He had learned to curse with great vehemence as a spectator in the smithy where the blacksmith gave him shelter, and kept his wings clipped. He was a very old bird when I was a boy, and was still on a rafter in the smithy when I was grown up and married with a family. He died before I could take my children to see him and was replaced by another bird obtained by the old smith's son, who felt that the smithy had to have a raven.

April 1978

THE wild cock pheasant now follows me about like a dog, blackmailing me to scatter handful after handful of layer pellets for him to stuff his crop.

The other morning he somehow materialised at my heel as I was going into the henhouse and clucked encouragingly when I stopped in my tracks to ask him where he thought he was going. We went back down to the hut, which was really what he wanted me to do, for I had no food with me at the time. I opened the hut and got yet another handful of pellets to scatter for him. He lost no time in picking up the pellets as soon as I had thrown them down, but while he was stuffing himself, one of the old brown hens, a heavy-footed, lumbering old biddy, arrived on the scene to get her share. The cock pheasant and the fluffed-up matron proceeded to fight. The pheasant flapped up and did his best to strike with his spurs. The old hen slashed with her beak, and the "dance" carried them away across the grass, whereupon the pheasant simply crouched for a moment and came arrowing back to the place where the pellets were still waiting for him. The hen was thoroughly out-manoeuvred and consequently lost interest.

The following morning I had made up my mind to let the wild pheasant have as much as he could take before the hens were let out, expecting him to wander off and digest the contents of his crop somewhere in the undergrowth. This was not to be. A second cock pheasant, a handsome ringneck, had arrived on the scene. Instead of rushing towards me, the tame bird was intent upon giving battle to the intruder. They postured, threatened, fluttered, crouched again and ignored my presence completely. The confrontation continued all morning and for a good part of the afternoon. Late in the day I could see that the real owner of the territory had managed to establish his right to it. I fed him just before he went up into the pines to roost. He was very hungry the day after the battle. I could hear his rival making a challenge from the adjoining field, but he didn't come over the wall and make a second attempt to take over.

April 1978

NO kind of woodland sound delights my ear more than the hammering of a woodpecker using a dead tree as his sounding board. What the message is defeats me, but a Lorenz or Seligmann might have the answer, and perhaps have the ear capable of picking up the reply rapped out by some other happy woodpecker in a wood a mile away. That the woodpecker isn't intent upon chopping his way into the tree is obvious to the observer who manages to locate the source of the sound. It is too easy to suggest that when the woodpecker turns his head, he is listening simply for the movement of the insect buried in the rigid, dead tree. I am inclined to think that the insect, the beetle or whatever it is, might not scuttle away in the tunnels of darkness it inhabits, but stand petrified as humans sometimes do when there is a loud knock on their door late at night.

If this is anthropomorphic, I apologise. It is anthropomorphic to see the woodpecker's turning of his head first to right and then to left as if testing one ear against the other, or trying to pick up a message from his left or right side. It is enough that it is a fascinating sight. I can stand and admire the bird as something very specially adapted to the life it leads, with those large, gripping feet, the pick of a beak, the stiff, splayed-out tail to balance the dumpy body vertically on the trunk of the tree. I admire them, green or spotted. I love the way the yaffle loops out of the wood and across the field. He makes my hackles stand with his mad laughter. I admire his moss greenness and his blood marking. I have never been able to get over

the hinged tongue and the length of this probing implement which, when he comes to the slate roof of the cottage, he deftly insinuates under slates to lick out larvae.

My daughter tells me that a builder who was making some renovations at her house was concerned to see and hear a woodpecker operating on the flagpole on his own property. Undoubtedly, he felt, the pole was rotten and would have to come down. Why else would the woodpecker be so intent upon hammering it? I felt that he was mistaken and that, since flagpoles are generally painted, the chances of the pole holding a feast for the woodpecker were slight. What was happening, I suggested, was that the woodpecker was transmitting a kind of woodpecker morse and receiving messages back.

I have noticed that when a woodpecker really wants to bore into dead wood the chips fly, and as a boy I used to look for these fresh borings around nesting time. A regular nesting hole is generally pretty impregnable and difficult of access, like the nest of a falcon. I remember finding one that couldn't be investigated without a long-handled spoon. My father, who discovered the spoon in my pocket, gave me a great lecture and made me promise to leave woodpeckers alone. He had a soft spot for them, and for most birds, although in his own boyhood he had treasured a collection of eggs which included that of a chough – the red-legged crow – a bird now even rarer than our smallest woodpecker, the lesser spotted.

May 1978

PERHAPS I should advertise myself as a tamer of birds? The wild, black-necked pheasant with his crimson wattles came to my hand a month ago and now follows me about like a dog until I feed him. He needs breakfast and supper, and will come like an arrow from any corner of the ground to greet me and have his hand-out – an ounce or two of layer pellets which he bolts down, pecking furiously between times. When he has stuffed his neck he pauses and looks rather over-full for a minute before he waggles his head a bit, working the dry material down into his crop as though swallowing his Adam's apple, an organ he doesn't possess. At close range I know his expression well. I have described him in detail to my wife. The other day I told her how the wattled, red area of his face was increasing. I had been forced to conclude that such a thing happens when a bird is maturing and gets his full breeding plumage, and yet it was all rather too much for even my own vivid imagining.

That I was in a Box and Cox situation didn't strike me. How could there be two cock pheasants, both black necks, both newly come to feed from my hand and identical in every detail, except for this red wattle detail that could come and disappear, for this morning this is what happened! I fed the pheasant at about eight o'clock. He stuffed himself full, went up the slope and stood among the daffodils and flapped his wings and crowed. I smiled at him, pleased to see the brilliant sheen on his head and shoulders and thinking how much good food improves the condition of a bird. That was that. A friend called and we talked and I showed him some colour pictures I had taken of this newly tamed cock, picking food close to my foot, and with an empty cartridge case thrown in to remind me of my long-ago wicked ways. A moment later, I suddenly heard the pheasant making his clucking sound and my friend came to the window to see me give the beggar his second hand-out.

While I was feeding the bird I looked him in the face. Full-frontal reveals that his redness bridges his beak. The bird I fed at eight, and the one in my picture, lacks this adornment. I have two tame pheasants, handsome cocks and almost identical in everything but that bridge-of-the-nose crimson adornment. I can't get over it, but it is so. One lives up in the wood and the other comes over the wall from the wood down below us. I have photographic evidence of my pheasant-taming ability.

I begin to wonder what will happen next? Perhaps all the keeper's birds will come here for sanctuary. That would be a great laugh. The keeper used to invite me to a shoot once in a while.

SKETCHES OF BIRDLIFE

TALKING about birdwatching, I was fortunate the other day when I saw an avocet, a somewhat infrequent visitor to my part of the world and one that belongs, I think, more on the eastern side of the country. It was stalking gently along and occasionally scooping water with that wonderfully up-curved bill, and I don't think I have ever seen a more graceful bird in my life. I watched it from the car. It was on a saltwater flash along with half a dozen everyday gulls and waders, and it made my day.

I suppose exotic, rare and unusual birds stop us all in our tracks. I can remember almost having an accident when a kite happened to fly alongside the car on a forestry road in mid-Wales, and kept pace with us for perhaps 100 yards before swinging away and rising in the air. An osprey once fished in front of me on an Anglesey lake and battered through the water with something he caught, while I caught nothing at all. I told someone about its presence on this particular water and the following day the poor bird was driven off by people wanting to film him. I said nothing about the golden eagle that wafted past me in Galloway, although I later discovered its presence was an open secret.

It doesn't pay to advertise what one sees, whether by word of mouth or by writing about it in the press, for there are some very determined people who will pursue their quarry as relentlessly as any man ever hunted a wild animal.

July 1979

A KIND of pecking order must apply among birds of all species. A herring gull is a fair-sized bird, although it may weigh only a few ounces. It is an imposing creature and looks well able to take care of itself when confronted with smaller scavengers, but at heart it is timid if not cowardly.

The other day I watched one of our resident herring gulls struggling to cope with a string of pork rind I had put down for the bantams before letting them out. The gull tried to sort the titbit before gobbling it lengthwise, and a pair of jackdaws, evidently realising that they must nip in at top speed or the gull would bolt the crackling, flapped in the face of the gull and drove it off so that they could seize the morsel. Greed made both of them take hold, and the string of pork was dragged first this way and then that, until the two daws were confronted by a bouncy magpie who seemed to give them a hard-eyed look as he took the thing away from them. He was in the air, with the rind hanging from his beak, when a carrion crow swooped and made him drop it. The rind fell into a stand of nettles into which the crow decided he wouldn't descend, and that was the end of it.

The magpie perched in a tree. The crow sailed back up to the wood. The jackdaws sat on the roof of the hut apparently waiting for another tasty morsel to appear. The gull flew slowly round and round, seemingly dazed by it all. Dog-in-the-manger, it sometimes strikes me, is what living is about. Perhaps a mouse got the titbit in the end.

SKETCHES OF BIRDLIFE

AS one gets older, I am inclined to think that nostalgia is promoted by more and more things one encounters that bring recollections of a world that used to be. In the past few years I have seen the nightjar only once or twice and can't think when I heard it *churring* until last week when I was coming away from the lake as the light was beginning to go. The lake was still. One could hear a fish rising half a mile down the water. The nightjar calling stopped me in my tracks. I was back in my yesterdays, when I not only seemed to have listened to it through all my summers, but watched its airy flight after moths that earned it the name of moth-owl.

The Welsh countryman had his own names for the nightjar – *bran nos*, the night crow, *gwenol y nos*, the night swallow, though he more often called it *nyddyr*, the spinner, or the spinning-wheel bird because of the sound it made. Goatsucker is one of the nightjar's commoner names in other parts of Britain, but my record of Welsh names doesn't include this one, or any reference to the goat. Puckeridge was another of its names mentioned by T. A. Coward, and this, I would suggest, had Irish origins, for puck is the Irish word for goat.

The nightjar, according to one authority, arrives in my part of the world in mid-May and is gone by the end of September. I remember one of my grandfather's men coming back from an expedition up to the moor, with a nightjar he had knocked down with a throwing stick. The killer of the nightjar was soundly berated for his crime, not because anyone thought very much about the scarcity of nightjars at that time, for the summer evenings were filled with the sound of their purring, but because this was a "corpse" bird and to kill one would bring bad luck.

On a previous occasion I saw the bird flying away from the bottom of the cliff here. It seemed to be hawking moths. My attention was drawn to it by the clap of its wings, a slightly sharper sound than that made by a woodpigeon. Nostalgia is as much in sound as in scent. The nightjar was somewhere up on the rocky ridge half covered with heather and stunted fir trees and both scent and sound took me back at least half a century.

September 1979

LIVING in isolation one may talk to various animals without being heard by a neighbour and dubbed an eccentric. I do it all the time and the response I get is fascinating.

The other evening the season's hatch of tawny owls, now fledged and inhabiting the pines, was somewhere in the trees immediately above the court. My wife drew my attention to a particular bird and out I went to talk to it. My usual conversation with tawny owls is by the use of a series of *hoo-hoos*, produced by putting my hands together in front of my mouth and breathing heavily into them to make this noise. I did my best and saw the owl lean forward and cock his head in a manner somewhat similar to the hens, but he was a youngster. Instead of replying with a *hoo-hoo*, as many other visiting owls have done in the past, he made a clacking sound, which both owls and hawks sometimes make when they are uneasy, and then replied with a *twit-twit* which I chose to disregard. I made my favourite sound again and a bird somewhere higher up said *twit-twit* with a certain urgency. I was evidently on the wrong wavelength altogether.

There was no more conversation, but I distinctly saw the bird on the limb stretch his wing to the side and raise a foot before he took to the air and flapped silently through the trees into the deeper shadows of pines up near the face of the cliff. I had been trying to talk to juveniles of course. Later on, in the moist evenings of late autumn, I shall probably talk to these owls and get a more civil reply.

October 1979

I HAVE been thinking about the sounds of yesterday, having received a letter or two about the corncrake. A few, particularly fortunate and well-placed people, not only still hear the crake but see it, which pleases me enormously for the expressway and the touring caravans, the "alpine coach" and the peregrinations of sightseeing man in general have all but banished the bird from these parts.

A friend who lives in Roehampton writes to say that he and his wife saw four, probably two pairs, on the Ayrshire-Wigtownshire border on his annual visit to Galloway. Another reader, venturing much further north, to South Harris, wrote to tell that this year he saw the bird walking through a small flock of hens kept by the owners of the hotel at which he was staying. Subsequent to this visit my correspondent had a letter from the owner of the hotel to say that their labrador had caught a corncrake and was encountered with only the legs of the bird showing from his mouth. The unfortunate crake was rescued, the dog evidently being particularly soft-mouthed, restored to its personal comfort and allowed to fly off, which it did, croaking its indignation. This happened, in fact, just before a member of the Royal Family visited the hotel for lunch. It could have been, suggests my correspondent, that the labrador considered he had produced a delicacy HRH might appreciate. The crake was, of course, once commonly shot where it was discovered and found its way on to the page of the gamebook in Colonel Hawker's day.

November 1979

afterwards that it was an emergency stop-over when hard weather was on the way. "Here," said the leader, "out of the east wind. It's the best place for the moment." It hasn't happened again, and I am not sorry, for who wants a starling roost?

That particular evening the murmuration went to a crescendo and died with scarcely a twitter afterwards. The outsize flock moved away without a sound in the morning, just the whirring of wings as they ascended and swept off like a smoke cloud. Yesterday I watched a similar flock come past and go on to the fields of the farm below, but they were almost skittish in their landing, for moments later they rose again and flew low over the adjoining countryside and went higher as they headed towards the river. I could imagine them finding a bed of reeds and taking refuge there for the night.

THE only time I have seen starlings in close proximity to the cottage was one very severe winter when they came in their hundreds, settling down in a corner where the path goes up the side of the cliff between some deciduous trees and our pine wood. Their descent on that particular occasion was like a cross-section of a whirlpool, a great vortex of circling birds sweeping down to just a few trees. We are under cliff, and almost wooded in, so that starling flocks sweep on towards the more open country to the south-west. On that long ago occasion they exercised the telepathic magic that makes a starling flock turn or descend, and down they came to stay with us. They stayed only one night, and I thought

The starling has always fascinated me by the industrious way it covers the ground when feeding, and by the sheer delight it displays in the morning sunlight when it sings itself into a frenzy. When I was a child I used to have a pigeon loft to which my birds had access through draining tiles built into the gable. One year starlings came in to occupy the wall top where rafters made divisions along the length of the loft. Three lots of birds nested. They were noisy and aggressive, and when the young were hatched the untidy nests became infested with fleas. The place had to be cleared out and fumigated when they left. Fortunately that one season was enough and the pigeons had the place to themselves the following year.

SKETCHES OF BIRDLIFE

CONFESSION is good for me, and I confess to being not so much a television addict as the kind of person who weakly sits down to be put to sleep by a load of old rubbish.

I sometimes wonder what the cat thinks of it. She, too, allows herself to be put to sleep by the box. I suspect that more people sleep through television than watch it, and there is something significant in the fact that one never sees cures for insomnia advertised in television commercials.

I have often heard of dogs and cats settling down in front of the box. Both my cat and my dog did so, and dozens of readers have written to tell me about their cats and dogs viewing things like Starsky and Hutch and other celebrated soporifics. It isn't often one hears of a duck that stops to look at the box, but a reader wrote to me about a duck that did this the other day, and, apparently, had no compunction about trespassing in order to do so.

"This evening," says my correspondent, "I was leaving this short road in this small market town in my old Land-Rover and before I reached the main road I saw a duck in the light of my headlamps. I stopped before the main road and switched off the engine, wondering how to deal with the situation. A thought came to me – call on Miss Jasmine, who has lived here longer than I have and has a house on the corner. Miss Jasmine, a resourceful person, said she would open her garden door so that I could drive the duck in. It was, she said, a mus-covy and it belonged to the vet who lives on the opposite side of the main road.

"My first attempt to do as Miss Jasmine suggested was not successful and the muscovy took off over my shoulder. Perhaps he sensed that Miss Jasmine's cat was not far away. Our next attempt was successful, however, and we got the duck into the garden and closed the door. The duck had waddled in and after a search we found him, sitting down on the carpet in Miss Jasmine's front room – watching television. We closed the door and telephoned the vet who was not long in coming over. He said, 'Oh, it's you, Fred. What are you doing out so late?' A short walk across the carpet and Fred was safely under his owner's arm."

My correspondent didn't say what kind of programme the duck was watching. It might have been one of those wildlife things, but not, surely, an advertisement for deep-freeze duckling?

June 1981

SOME years ago I corresponded with a gentleman who had set himself the task of recording birdsong and producing sheet music of birds such as the bullfinch and the blackbird. He would from time to time send me his minor score, which, knowing I had no musical talent, he hoped I might have played to me. I still have the violin I was given as a boy, but it stubbornly refused to respond to my efforts; and birdsong, even for amateurs, was beyond my ability.

I have often felt that what I should really have done was to go out and make tape recordings of bird songs that please me. There is no way that the music made by the wren or the yellowhammer, the blackbird or the goldfinch can be conveyed alphabetically. I find that when ornithologists describe the notes of birds it is almost impossible to relate their alphabetical sequences to the real thing, perhaps because pitch and tonal quality and the range of my own hearing are involved. A good musician with a string instrument might give a reasonable imitation of what might be called the twittering of a wren. The song of the ascending lark would be more difficult.

The call of the corncrake is adequately conveyed by the word crake, and the old word for the crow – *ki-ah*, as it was called by country people in Galloway when I was a child – was the nearest thing to the cry of the bird. Songbirds, however, don't always sing their full song but sometimes tune up and trill, giving us phrases from their repertoire. One discovers a bird in full song in a summer downpour, and the sheer ecstasy of the performance can root one to the ground. It requires a particular dedication to the subject to appreciate that there are singers and singers in the bird world, just as there are great and lesser lights on the stage.

The poet's thrush "at the corner of Wood Street" sang to the sunrise and delighted its audience. A wren sometimes sings in our wood like that, and to tell other people what that small song does to me is as impossible as it is to explain what I feel when I listen to the music of Bach, Chopin or Mozart. W. H. Hudson, incidentally, found himself baffled by Darwin's lack of enthusiasm for the birdsong of species encountered in Patagonia. Perhaps what he was really saying was that Darwin, brilliant naturalist though he was. didn't have a great feeling for bird music.

SKETCHES OF BIRDLIFE

ALL my idle days would fill several books if I were to recall them in print. Sometimes I am overcome with a sense of guilt at having pottered away my time, here and there, while the kind of man who my father and my grandfather cited as a proper example of a well-spent life jets here and there, influencing the destiny of man.

I find myself thinking this way after a whole day spent on a boat on a reed-fringed, weedy lake watching a pair of swans and a family of cygnets paddling in line, and a coot making a little grebe uncomfortable by seeing it off when it happened to venture near its nest. The beauty of rowing boats is that they don't pollute the air and make no more noise than the oarsman generates when he mishandles his blades. I am not the world's best oarsman, but I drift rather well. I drifted down on the

family of swans. The adult birds threatened with hunched wings. The cygnets weren't in the least worried and came right alongside to see what I was up to. The coot headed for me at once, and I wasn't sure whether he was coming for food or defending his territory.

Away under an overhanging bush his mate was perched on a raft-like nest of green reed stalks, a structure more like one built by a grebe than a coot, who generally favours dead rushes. The little grebe dived and bobbed up ever so often. When it came up nearer the coot's nest the male coot came rushing across the water, paddling on the surface like a water-skier making a last desperate effort to avoid sinking. The grebe did what he is expert at doing, and dived again. The coot went off to trail back another green stalk for his mate. The female probably found this tiresome for she had to make frequent readjustment of the nest pile. The male seemed to while away his time going for another and then another stem of reed.

I had nothing else to do but watch. The wind ruffled the surface of the lake, picking up green platters of water lily once in a while. Two herons came beating over, but when they saw me raised themselves up over the tallest of the trees on the bank, making me think they must have been assailed with shot more than once. They didn't come down to see if they could get a fish from the weeds. I didn't get one either, in the afternoon or the evening, but as my companion said as we went home, such a day restores the soul.

February 1982

NOSTALGIA and the sounds of rooks in a rookery in spring are synonymous as far as I am concerned, having lived in an area without a rookery for more than 20 years. I can hardly imagine an estate agent including a rookery as one of the amenities of a property he is trying to sell, for not everyone would delight in the sound of rooks battling over nesting materials.

In my case, however, it might just swing the balance. I was brought up as a child with rookeries close at hand. Later on we had one in our old village, and the sound of rooks in spring was to me like the drone of bees in summer. There were other sounds I loved as much – the bleating of young lambs and the call of the lapwing or green plover in March – but rookery activity transfixed me. I could watch rooks for hours without ever becoming bored.

The thing begins almost imperceptibly with the renovation of old nests. This activity occupies a few birds in the very early days of the new year, and increases until it occupies a colony that suddenly become vociferous and jealous of one another. The disputes and the skirmishes go on and on. Sticks are fought over. Birds come tumbling down from the tops of trees locked in aerial combat until they are within a few feet of the ground. All this is watched quite objectively by other rooks who remain perched and apparently unconcerned about the rights and wrongs of the thing. People are often like that. When the business is settled there may be harsh comment or an occasional flare-up of temper, but a rookery is where the young are raised, and feeding them is a pretty full-time job. Afterwards come those daily flights to the arable fields.

I used to enjoy rooks going out in the morning as much as I did watching them when they were occupied with intensive care for the young. What governs the morning flight may be light and wind direction, but it is always a foraging expedition and its direction is decided upon soon after the colony is in the air. There may be, for all I know, rook scouts, just as there are scout bees to find a source of nectar and summon the colony to the feast. I used to watch the occupants of one particularly large colony swirling and milling round the rookery for minutes on end, the birds as excited and as talkative as a football crowd. Then having decided which way they were going, they would fly off like a column of smoke before a breeze, their happy conversation audible for as much as a mile.

What telepathy is involved I don't know, but as a boy I could believe that a message was passed, as it seemed to be in a flight of hurrying starlings or an echelon of grey geese. I miss this kind of thing now.

SKETCHES OF BIRDLIFE

YESTERDAY there was a sound of knocking, which seemed to indicate that we had a caller, although how he or she failed to notice that we had sizeable door-knockers on both doors, as well as the ding-dong bell, I couldn't imagine. I was busy at the typewriter and called to my wife, "There's somebody at the door!" Shortly afterwards she informed me that there had been no one at the door or, if there had been, he had gone away.

I was puzzled. People who come all the way up here are usually more persistent. All might have been forgotten except that it happened again. The knocking, four or five sharp knocks, sounded through the house. I checked in case there was an airlock in the cold water pipe, for it sometimes hammers a bit, but there was no response when I turned on the cold water.

Today I was at the typewriter, once more, when the knocking resumed. Could it be my wife's favourite ghost, the grey lady she had once seen here? Could it be my father protesting about something? It seemed overhead now. Reluctantly I went to see who, or what, was up there on the roof knocking and seeking admission. Our caller peered down at me. It was a newly arrived green woodpecker who had been hammering away in one of the lead gulleys. Well, so long as we know what it is, and he doesn't peck a hole in the lead, he is welcome. It is some comfort to know that the grey lady isn't lurking about and father lies content in his grave.

August 1982

A FLIGHT of long-tailed tits, which I felt would soon be dispersing to pair up and nest, came hurrying down the cliff and into the tree-tops above the cottage. I was puzzled at the way they came until a sparrowhawk, a sleek and fast-flying female, swept over the bushes on a level with the tops of the pines where they stand below the rock face. Nothing jinks and negotiates through trees better than the round-winged hawks, but the long-tailed tits had been through all this before and sheltered in the bushy extremities of the Corsican pines.

The sparrowhawk passed them and came back again, half-hovering, peering this way and that but deciding that she couldn't really pick them out of the kind of cover into which they had gone.

She sailed out and waited on for a little while, swept right over the pines once again, and then went leisurely down to the trees beyond the lane. If she found prey there she certainly didn't come back to harry the unfortunate long-tailed tits. They turned aside and went unobtrusively along the cliff face, keeping in the shelter of the pines until they got into deciduous trees further along. There a great network of fine twigs and branches would have screened them from the sparrowhawk, had she come in pursuit. They no doubt went on, right out of this particular hawk's territory. This sort of hazard lies in wait for birds as they migrate before the breeding season.

A LETTER from a correspondent made me think about the problems of coping with the rehabilitation of an injured swallow. My correspondent had been distressed to find one of these birds in the clutches of his cat. As I would have done, he rushed to rescue it.

"We have a whole squad of swallows which nest in our village hall gables," he writes, "and sadly they regularly collide with overhead telegraph wires, are wounded and fall to the ground where they are easy prey to the cats. I have tried in vain to restore to health both swallows and swifts, but as they feed on the wing I have constantly failed and the birds have all died. Imagine my joy, when, after nursing this bird most of the night and snuggling it into my pyjamas, I managed to persuade it to fly the following day. It appeared to me that, once airborne again, with a high-pitched call it circled over the garden in thanks – imagination perhaps, but we were overjoyed."

I am inclined to think that a lot of people who try to rehabilitate birds in similar circumstances, and particularly those that have been seized by a cat, are much too concerned to feed the victim when all it needs is peace in which to recover from shock. A shoebox with a lid, and perhaps something on which the terrified bird can lie, is all that is needed. Let it have time to recover before handling it. The more robust species will generally advertise the fact that they are ready to go by flapping about in the box. Delicate birds have to be handled very gently.

SKETCHES OF BIRDLIFE

THEY say that too much bathing weakens a man, but birds love a bath. When I cut down a cypressus on the edge of the lawn to give more light in the kitchen, I made sure the base was sawn level because it seemed the perfect place for a birdbath. There was such a thing close at hand, a stone vessel over 18 inches in diameter and three inches deep. Only the tiny blue tit seemed to have difficulty in taking a bath, flitting towards the water and turning back at the last minute after immersing only one leg and finding the bath too deep. The larger birds walked in, thrushes, blackbirds, chaffinches, sparrows, greenfinches and, believe it or not, a full-grown woodpigeon who puffed himself up and sat there like Colonel Blimp in some fashionable Turkish establishment.

There is as much competition for the bath as in a seaside boarding house. The starling sees off the thrush. The finches are held back by a pair of loutish sparrows that try to keep the whole thing for their exclusive delight until something bigger swoops down. Some birds take a positive delight in splashing water all over themselves, and when they have gone the water level is reduced to a point where even the blue tit may stand up to his thighs and give himself a swill down. I go out with the watering can and after rinsing the bath refill it to the brim. This exercise, like replenishing the food on the birdtables, is watched from afar, and the minute I have withdrawn a thrush or blackbird will be down to enjoy the fresh water before Tom, Dick and Harry get in to leave tidemarks. Being on rising ground as we are, there can't be many places within perhaps half a mile where birds can find either drinking water or bathing facilities, and in the recent spell of hot weather the birdbath has had as many customers, I would think, as the nearest municipal bath.

January 1984

ALTHOUGH I have often watched both the green and great spotted woodpeckers, neither of them very rare birds in a garden, I haven't watched them both at once. Yesterday, this was a rare treat, for while I was trying to locate the spotted fellow in his favourite oak on the side of the lawn, and craning my neck because foliage on the tree made it very difficult to find him, out of the corner of my eye I saw the yaffle landing on the grass.

What a front-heavy, pickaxe character the green woodpecker is, progressing in hops across the turf and searching for the ant colony. Spotted wood-peckers seem to avoid settling on the ground but are more acrobatic in their movements, especially when, at the birdtable, they hang on to a tube of nuts.

The spotted woodpecker in the oak tree was ham-mering away when I discovered him. My neck had become stiff from peering upwards, but once I found him I could follow his progress up the tree-trunk. He hammered for a minute or two and then moved up to hammer again. It seemed to me he was flushing something out from dead bark on spurs of the tree, the ends of which had long since broken off. The hedge prevented me from seeing exactly what he was doing, but he wasn't boring a hole, nor was he drumming for the benefit of other woodpeckers. He was lunching.

From his vantage point he must have seen the greenfinches clustering on tubes of nuts on both birdtables and decided that only fools and horses work, for he looped down for the free lunch, frightening the smaller birds away. The green woodpecker had by this time found a small rise on the lawn and was hammering into it. Perhaps there were ants' eggs in the mound as he appeared to be extracting something with the help of his particularly long tongue. Neither woodpecker paid the slightest attention to the other. Perhaps they don't recognise the other species at all. Finally the green one took wing and went looping away to the wood. The spotted stayed to fill up on nuts and then returned to the oak.

February 1984

HAVING abandoned my daily log of visitors to the birdtables I still keep watch for newcomers like the willow tit and the marsh tit, both of which made short visits to the feeding area, picking up morsels from the ground without alighting on the tables themselves. The marsh tit is a most handsome little bird, distinguishable from the willow by its glossy head. The willow tit, with a duller cap, has a light feather edging on its wing covers, but one bird may be mistaken for the other when they nervously flit in and away again. Had I continued with my daily list the total would have gone over 20 on at least two occasions, but the less bold willow and marsh tits were only casual callers.

The greenfinches, had I been recording individual numbers, would sometimes have been top of the list, for I have counted as many as ten either feeding or fluttering round the nuts. Most days we have three pairs of greenfinches on the table, consuming more peanuts than all the small birds put together. I take satisfaction from this.

If I sustain and nourish these handsome finches through the winter, and they can find enough to keep them when their natural food becomes available, we should have finer greenfinches. Certainly we shall have encouraged and carried the tits through winter, and we have all three of the common, gregarious species, blue, coal and great tit.

March 1984

LONG before the first snowdrop or crocus bloomed, I began to hear the first tentative twitterings and warblings of birds that frequent the tables here. It isn't so much a day or two of mild weather that persuades songsters to tune up for the dawn chorus, but a brightening of the light. This daily improvement lifts the spirit, even when the general tone of the day may be overcast by lingering rainclouds. Blue tits begin to skirmish more determinedly. The robin tries his few bars of music. Even the croak of the crow changes in tone, and the cock pheasant, shepherding unwilling hens, clucks to them like a domestic cock courting his favourites. At the same time the plumage of the birds becomes brighter, as though they had all been "done over" by Gould or Thorburn. The magpie's iridescence shows. His blue-black feathers seem to glow in the morning sun. The jay's wing is more distinctly blue and white, and what might have been dull brown becomes chestnut, or as near as makes no difference.

The sheen of condition is on them all, from the beautiful little marsh tit to the crow. They don't need to be told that February is gone and spring is here when March is done. I find the nuthatch looking more sleek, and the bullfinch, fat and round in his new paint, as handsome as any bird that ever perched in an apple tree. He is back here now, waiting, I can believe, for the apple blossom to break, although this won't happen for a long time yet. It is spring, so far as I am concerned, when the rooks begin their nest repairs, or I see a blue tit popping in and out of an old nest-hole.

SKETCHES OF BIRDLIFE

A PERSON who rescued a mallard's brood from the public highway arrived at our door the other evening with a great basketful of half-grown ducks to prove me wrong. I hadn't said a word to discourage her when she asked my advice about what to do with the ducklings, but I had implied that she hadn't much chance of success. I thought she would have to put herself out rather a lot. She had, for she had given the ducklings the run of the bathroom, and the bath in particular, which you might say was going overboard completely!

There had been one casualty, and I suppose a wild brood might have been similarly depleted. The survivors were taken to a wildfowl sanctuary, but I have a feeling that if, in another year, a motherless brood comes on to the road the lady concerned will pass by on the other side. My visitor left, and the following morning we had a letter from a friend who had faced a similar situation with house martins. Now the trouble with insectivorous birds is that their food is minute and much too elusive for them to be hand-fed. In this case the house martin's nest, complete with nearly ready-to-fly youngsters, dropped from the eaves of the house. Compassion is overpowering in some people. Our friend couldn't think what to do and, hastening to get advice, was finally persuaded to put nest and nestlings in a shoebox on a window-sill, hoping the parents would come and attend to the young in this new situation. Shortly after the box was in position the adult house martins managed to get all but one of their offspring to fly, but

it looked as though the youngster that remained in the shoebox was doomed to die.

The following morning, the adult house martins returned to feed the last of the brood. Before the day was out, it, too, managed to take wing, flying into a nearby bush. After a minute or two the young bird stretched and fluttered its wings and launched itself to fly around with those already on the wing. Perhaps all it needed was to be launched. I have often performed this service for grounded swifts whose shoulder muscles were too weak to enable them to beat themselves into the air. House martins and swallows are, of course, of a different design, and have legs better suited to pedestrian activity and take-off from a horizontal surface.

SKETCHES OF BIRDLIFE

WITHOUT starlings the world would be a less enjoyable place as far as I am concerned, for individually and collectively they are the most fascinating birds. Yesterday there were three around the birdtable, probably members of a family hatched either in a hole in the broken-topped birch tree or in the birdbox I fastened to the stump of a tree that came down last winter. Why weren't these lingering, odd birds not picked up by the great flock of starlings that went like the tail of a comet or a thunderball across the sky on the previous day? Are there always a few contracted-out starlings that fend for themselves on local pastures or the gardens of suburbia?

Even more intriguing is the thought of flocks in the making. The swirl of birds that goes suddenly down to a roost is obviously a company that has been gathering numbers for weeks or months. Starlings, like jackdaws, are gregarious even if they spread out to nest. Where the pickings are good, large numbers (amalgamations one might call them) clear vast acreages of ground of all kinds of insects harmful to the arable farmer's enterprise and sometimes deadly to the flockmaster.

The group moves on, sometimes before harder weather petrifies the grass and the ground in which their food lives. Perhaps they have sensors that tell them when to go or they travel ahead of a cold airstream on one migration and behind a warm one on another? What it is about only a scientist who has made a study of these birds could say. For my part I love to see them coming in to roost, coiling like smoke, streaming in on a broad front, rising for a minute and then breaking up almost to crash land in the branches of their chosen trees.

Yesterday, before the main flock passed over, a minor one arrived and made a fast circle of our wilderness where one or two large dead trees stand out. Either they took this as a likely roost or a temporary rest for the main flock, or they were just waiting for the larger one to catch up. But they came down, almost tumbling out of the sky and perched in clusters like black fruit on the two dead trees. They were up and away as soon as the mass flight passed. I watched them whirring desperately to catch up, which I am sure they did before nightfall.

SKETCHES OF BIRDLIFE

APART from the wintering woodpigeons, the commonest flocking bird hereabouts at the moment seems to be the peewit, whose winter flight is as heavy and laborious now as it is light and airy in spring. I have always had a soft spot for the peewit or lapwing, one of the commonest birds of both pasture and arable land when I was a child. So common were they that if the ploughmen were told to lift and replace eggs they found on the field, they complained that they were wasting time. They were, of course, for only rarely did the peewit accept what was supposed to be her nest on the turned furrow. Nevertheless we had men who diligently obeyed the instruction. Almost always the peewit laid another clutch and her young escaped before the ground was harrowed and rolled after sowing.

The spring cry of the peewit took the place of the cry of the wild goose, for by the time the flocks of lapwings had broken up, the geese had gone north. In winter the geese call as they cross the sky, but the lapwings are silent. Both may graze on the same kind of shoreline pasture, but keep to themselves as the flocks of curlews do. It is a matter of pace. The curlews are busy, while lapwings spend a lot of their time standing like china ornaments laid out in a market.

These winter flocks have diminished in number since my childhood. Certainly some of the farms I knew as a boy have no nesting peewits at all now where once great baskets of eggs were legally gathered without numbers ever diminishing.

BIRDS behave not unlike humans when they are house-hunting. They look round without serious intention of exchanging contracts. They peer in and depart and come back again, the way the blue tits and great tits behaved when I fixed the birdbox to the tall stump of the birch tree on the lawn. The starlings, however, would have liked to move in right away, and would have done so had the entrance permitted.

They discouraged lesser birds, and hammered away on the door like woodpeckers until I took the box down and enlarged the entrance. This happened two years ago. For two seasons the box has been tenanted by starlings. When the birds depart, tits go in and out to clean up the spiders and larvae that starling litter invariably supports.

I always had a feeling that, although I had remedied the defect of too small an entrance, the box was hardly big enough for a family of four young starlings. But we had a phenomenal hatch of young starlings on the lawn, chaperoned by at least four nesting pairs. My birdbox, though, probably accounted for only two young birds each season. It was obvious that my box on the stump was far too small. I have now built a new one, with a lid that can be removed for cleaning the thing out. It stands on the loggia roof, and already a starling has perched on it. It remains to be seen whether our tally of nesting starlings increases now or whether birds that occupied the box on the stump will move to brand new accommodation on the roof of the loggia.

September 1985

NOTICING a heron that really wanted to alight on the shore to stalk fish but was frustrated by the presence of people sporting themselves in company with their dog, I watched the grey bird perch in the trees on the far side of the water. The perch was a flimsy one and the wind rocked the ungainly bird, who was determined not to leave its favourite fishing place.

Herons tend to haunt certain productive stretches of water. I can remember one that would always rise from the same stretch of a burn. I would go, either to tickle the small trout, or look for a yellow-hammer's nest in the bushes along the bank and the heron would rise calling Frank's name. In those days I think the heron nested some miles away on rock ledges. Keepers discouraged them if they settled anywhere else much in the same way as they destroyed hawks, owls and waterhens. Now heronries are strictly protected and no one may shoot the bird.

I remember my elders displaying a positive hostility to the heron, although I was never told why. Perhaps they took their cue from the gamekeepers. I was warned, however, not to shoot the bird for it was capable of "foxing". It would appear dead and lie with its pick of a beak on its chest, but the moment an unwary man reached for it the beak would be used like a spear to stab its would-be killer and perhaps knock his eye out. I never shot one. I liked to see the heron rise from the burn and admired the way it wafted itself off with slow, ponderous wing-beats that nevertheless carried it

away at an amazing speed. On the reservoir some fishermen tut-tut about the heron when they find the remains of dead fish on the bank. I am only depressed when the heron goes, for then it may be that fish are going to remain down. If the heron gives up, I give up. Sometimes he has had his fill and leaves, highly pleased with himself, which is what any self-respecting fisherman should do when he has had a good day.

The heron in the tree didn't stay there. Intrusive birdwatchers sent him off into the sky, the sun lighting his wings and back as he beat higher and higher and decided where he would go to fish in peace.

SKETCHES OF BIRDLIFE

SIGHTINGS of the kingfisher have been more frequent here in the south than they were when I lived in North Wales, where kingfishers were not, I think, less numerous but more difficult to spot on the wilder stretches of rivers and streams that they frequented. Here I have seen more of it this summer than last year, which is fortuitous, for kingfishers didn't do well in the hard winter and cold spring. The setback will certainly be overcome by this time, because the kingfisher goes in for second broods and, I believe, will have young in the nest on some occasions well into the autumn. What surprises me about this lovely little fishing bird is that it will frequent most unlikely stretches of sluggish and obviously polluted water. This must be because stagnant water, unsuitable for fish life, nevertheless produces an abundance of insects, and the kingfisher, like the dipper, likes aquatic insects wherever they may be found. I remember being surprised to discover that the kingfisher sings: one sat on a branch one day, when I was dallying by a Welsh river spying on salmon in a pool, and proceeded to trill delightfully. Somehow I had never expected such a bird to sing, but there it was, singing to its mate who fluttered about in the branches of the same tree.

Coming away from the reservoir the other day, I thought to explore the overgrown ditch that passes for a trout stream running alongside the large open water and found, on the first barrier holding back the "stream", a perky kingfisher intent on preening. I was quite close to him before he saw me and darted off upwater under the overhanging brushwood. Somewhere along the bank I knew there would be one of those water-vole tunnels in which the kingfisher often nests.

Once, after seeing a kingfisher going in and out of a hole in the bank, I attempted to reach its nest, such as it is, but all that I got for my pains was a hand coated with green slime and tiny fishbones. Kingfishers, for all their fine feathers, live in squalor. The bird I watched preening probably needed to clean itself every time it ventured to feed its brood in the unsanitary tunnel in which young kingfishers spend the first days of their lives.

October 1986

LOOKING out of the bedroom window this morning, I saw six magpies sporting themselves on and under the white seat on the lawn. It was a game of tag, it seemed, for the birds bounced about, chasing one another round the seat, along the back-rest, under the arms, down on to the grass below, and back up on to the seat.

All animals love to play, and magpies are no exception. They tease and harass one another at times, enjoying the game as children enjoy chasing one another in the schoolyard. I watched for several minutes until one of the birds cocked its head, spotting me at the window, and that small movement alerted its companions immediately. As one the six flew out over the lawn to perch in the prunis that stands in the middle of the near-at-hand paddock. They had done with the game now.

Later that day I was on the reservoir, where four brick structures stand in the middle of the water, surrounded now by an area of stone exposed as the level of the reservoir, used to top a nearby canal, has fallen. A family of young herons were playing the same kind of game with one another, flapping after each other, flying on to the top of the brick-work and looking down at others still stalking each other round the structure and flapping uncomfortably as their feet stuck in the rocks. Herons at play are an amusing sight. Normally their behaviour is much more restrained and sedentary, but they do, at least when they are young, have fun with one another. Life isn't all waiting, watching and brooding.

THE starlings were back home on a visit to the nestbox on the birch-tree stump. They were perched, one on the top of the nestbox and the other on a low branch of the adjoining birch tree. The two birds brooded until the great spotted woodpecker arrived on the scene. They kept their eye on the woodpecker as he went round the birch stump, ascending gradually, taking insects or grubs from the bark.

Finally he came to within a foot of the nestbox and the starling on the roof looked down at him. I imagine a word or two passed, for the woodpecker made a dart upwards and the starling, intimidated, flew up on to the top of the stump. The woodpecker seemed determined to make a house search but the starling anticipated this and suddenly dived in through the door. The other bird in the birch tree alongside made a swoop on the woodpecker just as he reached the entrance to the nestbox. I imagine the bird inside must have threatened the intruder at the same time for he was forced to give ground and flipped over to the base of the tree on which the second bird had been perched. Both starlings now sat on the stump, while the woodpecker began his exploration of the adjoining tree. Perhaps he was proving to himself that he wasn't afraid of the two starlings, but after a minute he moved on to the next tree and ran up the bark before finally flying off.

The starlings relaxed, becoming rounder and less sleek. They were contemplative again. They had proved their right to the stump and the nestbox.

SKETCHES OF BIRDLIFE

FIRST it was the great spotted woodpecker who attempted to inspect the starlings' nestboxes without an order to view. Next came a pair of squirrels, and by chance the starlings were on the scene again. The dash and impudence of the squirrels made it seem more of a game than an attempt to take over. One squirrel came at top speed to the birch stump and posed on the bark looking upwards. The starlings dropped down from the adjoining tree and took up strategic positions. The second squirrel raced over the lawn and round the stump, and the two birds separated to keep an eye on the two tree rats. The posing one ran up the stump but stopped a yard short of the nestbox. The other squirrel ran round and round the trunk. Now you see him, now you don't.

The starlings set themselves to defend. One entered the box; the bird outside swooped as the first of the squirrels tried his luck, and forced the little monster to run back down the trunk and race for the adjoining tree. Forgetting that there was a starling to be accounted for, the second squirrel rushed up, intending to dive into the nestbox. The starling hit him on the head and he fell all the way to the ground. A moment later he was running for his life back across the lawn to the boundary hedge. His partner on the birch tree evidently decided that he, too, had better make himself scarce, and made a dash for the hedge. No such skirmishes take place over the nesting places in the gables of the house, or the hole in the birch tree that has been used for years, but both wooden nestboxes are fought over regularly.

TWO cock pheasants arrive on the scene to await the hand-out of bread for the hens that always haunt the airing green at the back door after day breaks. One is our resident cock bird who for a while began to look the worse for wear as his pinions and tail feathers dropped out. He had the scraggy appearance of a very old man with a three-day growth of beard. His neck feathers were falling out. I suppose he must have been a little self-conscious, for he stopped coming until his fine feathers began to grow again.

When he looked the better for his wash and brush up he brought a young bird with him, a half-grown cock, lean and hungry and quick to run. The rivalry one might have expected was missing. It seemed as though the old bird had taken the younger one under his wing. As the old cock crows, my elders would say, the young one learns, and the two birds are now almost inseparable.

The hens pay them no attention at all but get on with their demolition of brown bread, which they attack with great enthusiasm, eating out the centre of the slice and leaving the outer crust for the magpies. The two cock pheasants aren't greedy. They never crowd the females or attempt to steal from them. I imagine it will be a month or two before they take a look at one another and discover they are rivals. The situation will change. Brotherly love and companionship will go overboard and the young cock, disillusioned, will be forced to run for his life and live a solitary bachelor life in the wilderness, though his day will come.

ILLUSTRATION CREDITS

Leonora Box: 55, 135, 139, 140, 145, 148, 151, 159, 160

John Busby: 10, 20, 22, 25, 33, 34, 43, 46, 52, 60, 62, 75, 79, 92, 99, 104, 106, 114, 116, 123, 125, 154, 171, 177, 178, 186, 188

Jeanne Colville: 42, 67, 82, 126

John Francis (Linden Artists): 174, 181, 191, 193, 197, 198, 201

Ros Hewitt: 2, 13, 16, 19, 27, 28, 36, 40, 48, 162

Caroline Holmes Smith (Virgil Pomfrett Agency): 15, 30, 39, 45, 57, 69, 85, 96, 100, 102, 109, 113, 118, 121, 143, 153, 169, 185, 195

Delyth Jones: 64, 76, 87, 133, 137, 146, 157

Robert Morton (Linden Artists): 59, 70, 72, 80, 89, 90, 110, 130, 167, 173, 182, 202

Barbara Walker: 8, 50, 94, 128, 164